Hot&Cold

JEWELRY CONNECTIONS

how to make jewelry with and without a torch

Hot&Cold

JEWELRY CONNECTIONS

how to make jewelry with and without a torch

KALMBACH BOOKS

kieu pham gray

Kalmbach Books
21027 Crossroads Circle
Waukesha, Wisconsin 53186
www.Kalmbach.com/Books

Lettered step-by-step photos by Zim Photography. All other photography © 2014 Kalmbach Books.

The jewelry designs in *Hot & Cold Jewelry Connections* are the copyrighted property of the author, and they may not be taught or sold without permission. Please use them for your education and personal enjoyment only.

Please follow appropriate health and safety measures when working with materials and equipment. Some general guidelines are presented in this book, but always read and follow manufacturers' instructions. Every effort has been made to ensure the accuracy of the information presented; however, the publisher is not responsible for any injuries, losses, or other damages that may result from the use of the information in this book.

Published in 2014
18 17 16 15 14   1 2 3 4 5

Manufactured in the United States of America

ISBN: 978-1-62700-050-5
EISBN: 978-1-62700-062-8

Editor: Mary Wohlgemuth
Art Director: Lisa Bergman
Technical Editor: Annie Pennington
Photographer: James Forbes

Publisher's Cataloging-in-Publication Data
Gray, Kieu Pham.
    Hot & cold jewelry connections : how to make jewelry with and without a torch / Kieu Pham Gray.
        p. : col. ill. ; cm.
    Issued also as an ebook.
    ISBN: 978-1-62700-050-5
    1. Jewelry making–Handbooks, manuals, etc. 2. Metal-work–Handbooks, manuals, etc.
    3. Costume jewelry–Handbooks, manuals, etc. I. Title. II. Title: Hot and cold jewelry connections
TT212 .G73 2014
739.274

contents

Introduction 6

THE BASICS
Materials 8
Tools 10
Techniques 18

THE PROJECTS
Memento pendants 38

Kisses pendants 44

Pearl of Wisdom pendants 50

Flourish bracelets 54

Spinning rings 59

Pod pendants.. 67

Spiral Chain bracelets 74

Wishes rings 80

Harnessed pendants 85

Pendulum earrings 89

REFERENCE CHARTS 94

ACKNOWLEDGMENTS 95

FROM THE AUTHOR... 95

The need to share knowledge is insatiable to me. I love to share everything I know how to do, from teaching kindergartners how to save money as a Junior Achievement volunteer to teaching friends how to make Vietnamese food in my kitchen to my passion for jewelry making. I can't help myself. I do only things I love and believe in, and sharing my passions is the ultimate reinforcement.

Making jewelry out of metal offers a variety of ways to approach the same challenges. In this book, my focus is on how those pieces of metal are connected: with wire, metal tabs, and other cold connections, or with metal that's heated until it's molten to form a hot connection. My goal is to teach you about the materials, tools, and techniques so you can choose an approach that works for you.

ABOUT THIS BOOK

First we'll look at choices in metal and other materials you'll be using. Next I'll guide you through tools with an eye toward helping you choose how to invest your money. Then—on to the jewelry projects.

My projects are presented in pairs showing a cold-connected version and a hot (soldered) version. You'll easily be able to see the differences in connection techniques and their application. By presenting the options side by side, you can make an informed decision about how you'd like to work based on your own design aesthetics, your skill and comfort level, and the tools and materials you have available. Along the way, you will also learn to create different patinas, cut and form shapes, and create textures.

The Basics

materials
tools
techniques

The Basics: materials

You have a lot of choices when it comes to the type of metal to use in your jewelry. While most everyone loves the look of silver and gold, in today's market, the cost of these precious metals can be prohibitive, especially if you are just starting out making jewelry. I focus on using copper and some silver in this book.

METAL

Luckily, jewelry suppliers today offer less-expensive alternatives in sheet and wire form, such as copper, nickel, and brass. Your local plumbing and roofing outlets also may sell copper sheet. Most often, sheet metal is sold in 6" (15.2cm) increments, so with a single purchase, you're likely to end up with more than enough for several jewelry projects.

The thickness of sheet metal is indicated by the gauge system: the lower the number, the thicker the metal. Confused? You're not alone. This isn't intuitive; it's the opposite of what you'd think it should be.

For accents and freeform shapes, use 22- to 26-gauge so you can cut the metal with shears. I use 24-gauge most often for these types of pieces.

For focal and base pieces, I use 20-gauge, or sometimes the thicker 18-gauge. Large pieces like bracelets, bangles, and rings hold up better when made with thick metal.

→ TIP **When you purchase your sheet metal, write the gauge on it with a Sharpie. Nickel, sterling silver, and fine silver can look similar, so do yourself a favor and mark what metal it is too. Mark the sheets again as needed as you cut pieces off your supply.**

Many of the materials shown or suggested for use in this book can be interchanged. I may show a project made of copper, but if you prefer making it with nickel or silver, go for it! Consider using mixed metals within one jewelry piece or even taking apart vintage jewelry to add variety to your metal choices.

Purchased metal shapes (you can find hearts, ovals, stars, and many others) and brass stampings are a lot of fun to use. They lighten your workload and provide instant gratification.

Vintage reproduction stampings often have patina added to create an aged look. Be careful not to heat antiqued pieces with a torch if you want to preserve the patina.

WIRE

Wire is an integral part of metalworking. When starting a new concept, I like to test it using copper wire before using silver, and definitely before using gold! Because copper is inexpensive, I don't worry that I'm wasting costly supplies if things go wrong. Despite this, I save all of my scraps. Even an inch of scrap metal, whether wire or sheet, will be used at some time. Silver scrap is great for balling up into granules. I've even reused bent wire. And if it can't be reused, save it and turn in to your supplier for cash.

recycle it

Accents made from recycled jewelry can provide readymade texture and patina. Many of these pieces can be cut with wire cutters or bezel shears, filed, sanded, and easily attached with a cold connection. Because it's hard to know the metal composition of recycled findings, I recommend that you don't use them for soldered connections; plated finishes can burn off, or the metal itself can melt.

dead-soft or half-hard wire?

Consider how intricate the project is and how much control you need as you're bending the wire. Dead-soft wire has been annealed and is very malleable. Half-hard wire has been work-hardened through the milling process and has a lot of spring-back. I use half-hard wire when making earring wires. I use dead-soft wire to make rings and spirals because it will tighten to the shape I want with little spring-back.

wire gauge

Just as with sheet metal gauge, in wire gauge, the smaller the number, the thicker the wire. For comparisons in inches and millimeters, refer to the chart on p. 94, which uses the American Wire Gauge system.

I generally use the thickest wire I can work with for the project; thin wire becomes hard and brittle as you work it and can break. For projects such as binding and simple wrapping, 24-gauge is a good choice. When a wire component has to work to do (as a clasp or chain link, for example), I'll usually use 18-gauge; for a substantial focal piece, 16-gauge; for large rings, 10–12-gauge.

→ **TIP** Refer to the chart on p. 94 to check the availability of wire and sheet in various metals.

stocking your supply cabinet

In addition to sheet and wire, you'll need other findings and materials such as headpins, clasps, and chain to make metal jewelry. I suggest you keep a selection of materials and findings handy, starting with this shopping list and adding to it as you figure out your preferences:

❏ 6x6" (15.2x15.2cm) sheets of 24-gauge copper and brass
❏ 1x6" (25.5mmx15.2cm) sheets of 24-gauge sterling silver
❏ 12- to 26-gauge copper, sterling silver, and fine-silver wire, several feet of each
❏ sterling silver, gold-filled, and copper earring wires, 6 pairs
❏ sterling silver and gold-filled jump rings and headpins, 25
❏ silver-plated, gold-plated, copper, and brass headpins, 100
❏ silver-plated, gold-plated, copper, and brass jump rings, 50
❏ 2x2mm or 2x3mm copper or silver tubes, 24
❏ 24-gauge disks in copper, brass, and sterling silver in various diameters: .50", .75", and 1" (13, 19, and 25.5mm), 6 each
❏ sterling silver, copper, and brass clasps, 2 sets
❏ a selection of chain in sterling silver and copper
❏ a variety of metal shapes and vintage filigree shapes

→ **TIP** To save money, use copper or plated metal, especially for practice wire and headpins.

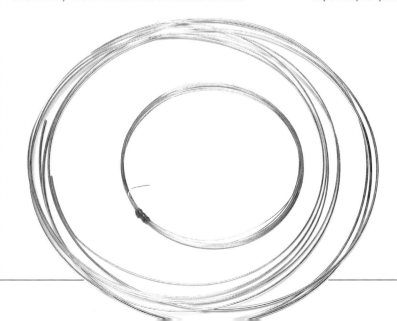

The Basics: **tools**

Building the right set of tools for jewelry making can seem overwhelming to a beginner, and the costs quickly add up. I believe in using what you have until it no longer works for you. As you begin, you may use tools found in your garage or at yard sales. By starting with what you have, you'll understand what you should buy next.

Quality in jewelry tools is usually directly related to cost. If you're going to buy all your tools new, buy the best that you can afford so that you don't end up replacing inferior tools. (This is especially true regarding wire cutters.) Use my lists as a guide, investing in the "must-have" list first. Later you'll read about additional supplies and setups you'll need for each technique.

MUST-HAVE TOOLS

For jewelry making, choose pliers with smooth surfaces inside the jaws. As you shop for pliers, consider ergonomic handles, milled edges to reduce marring of metal and wire, and pliers without springs to ease the tension on your hands.

If you need to practice with hardware-store pliers with teeth, place masking tape over the teeth or coat them with a product called Tool Magic to keep them from marring your work. If you replace the old pliers with new, keep the old pliers for odd tasks. Always use smooth-jawed pliers when you are doing wirework for finished jewelry.

wire cutters

Wire cutters should be your first real investment. Not all cutters are made the same; purchase the best that you can. If you have already bought an inexpensive pair, keep them as a spare for use when you don't care what happens to the blades. If you treat your cutters well and use them only on the wire they are intended to cut, they will last a lifetime. (Look inside the handles of the cutters or ask your supplier what gauge they can handle, and don't use your good cutters with steel wire or memory wire.) Look for ultra-flush cutters that create a flush cut on one side (the other side leaves a tapered cut) and a small head that's easy to maneuver in tight spaces.

roundnose pliers

Roundnose pliers have jaws that look like cones. They'll help you form round loops with wire. Top-of-the-line roundnose pliers will make your life easier, but an economy pair from the craft store or hardware store will work too. High-end roundnose pliers usually have small jaws, which allows you to make small loops for fine wirework.

chainnose pliers

Chainnose pliers can be found just about anywhere. The jaws are narrow at the tip to help you work in small spaces. From time to time, flatnose pliers will come in handy, but these three hand tools are must-haves from the start.

files

Begin with a #2 cut hand file. This big, relatively coarse file gets the work done quickly. Later, add a fine-cut mini file set for detailed work.

bezel shears, straight and curved

You'll use bezel shears to cut thin-gauge metal sheet. Most shears are rated for 20-gauge metal, although most people are not strong enough to shear this heavy of a gauge. Consider buying the best that you can afford and try before you buy, if possible, to determine which handle will be most comfortable for you.

metal hole punch

The easiest way to make a hole in metal is to use either a screw-down punch or a hand punch. However, there are other ways to create holes. Here are options from the least expensive to the most expensive, each with pros and cons:

1. **An aluminum handle from a bead reamer set and a twist drill bit.**
   Pro: You probably already own one.
   Con: Manual process.
2. **A pin vise and a twist drill bit.**
   Pro: Most come with a range of chucks that clamp the drill bits in place.
   Con: Another manual process.
3. **Screw-down punch.**
   Pro: The screw-down action of this punch is easy and efficient. You have a choice of two punch sizes.
   Con: The throats are shallow and may not reach as far as you'd like.
4. **Hand punch.**
   Pro: Easy to use. Cons: Leaves burrs; you're limited in size and thickness (24-gauge or thinner).
5. **A rotary tool (such as Dremel) or flex shaft and high-speed twist drill bit.**
   Pros: Fast; few limitations.
   Cons: Expensive; cumbersome.

nylon or rawhide mallet

Either mallet will work; it's your choice. These mallets shape and flatten metal without marring it.

bench block

You'll need a steel bench block as a hammering surface for stamping and forging metal. Choose the largest you can afford. Lightweight anodized aluminum blocks work for stamping and light-duty metalwork.

utility hammer

Almost any hammer—even an inexpensive one from the hardware store—will work as a general-purpose hammer. Make sure it's at least 8 oz. for use with metal stamps.

riveting hammer

This is a great general-purpose hammer. Use the cross-peen face to spread rivet heads and the flat face to flatten and finish the rivets.

center punches

Available in a variety of sizes, these tools look like metal pencils and are typically used for making divots in metal. We'll use them to make tube rivets. Choose one that is 1mm wider than the tubing you are using to rivet. Buy manual center punches; automatic center punches won't work for our purposes.

finishing punches

Finishing punches look like center punches, but they have a blunt end. They're usually used to drive nails, but we'll use them to finish rivets in hard-to-reach places. Choose sizes that fit the tubing you're working with (often 2–3mm diameter).

firesafe tweezers

You need these to handle hot metals during and after soldering; I have a straight version and one that's cross-locking. The insulated handles protect your hands. Don't use pliers; you risk melting the plastic handles or even burning your hands.

butane torch

To solder, you will need a torch. For starters, you can work with just about any butane torch, from a small crème brûlée torch to a torch made specifically for jewelry work. Until you work with large pieces of metal or get tired of refilling a small torch, the handheld butane torch will serve you well.

TOOLS TO ADD OVER TIME

There are many tools that can make your work a lot easier, but until you are more proficient or want to do more intricate work, you can begin without them. Add these tools over time as you need them or as you explore new techniques.

bench block #2

There are times when a second bench block will be handy; you can roll a piece of wire between them to straighten it, for example. Consider buying a 6x6" (15.2x15.2cm) block if you started with a 4x4" (10.2x10.2cm).

flex shaft

Although you can pierce, polish, and sand manually or with a rotary tool, the flex shaft is the power tool of choice for professional jewelers. If you're going to stick with jewelry making but do not already own a rotary tool such as a Dremel, I suggest you buy a flex shaft right off the bat.

Most flex shafts have adjustable chucks that hold small bits without a special adapter as you would need for a rotary tool. Begin with an assortment of these bits: a high-speed twist drill (.25–2mm), a mounted brass brush, a mounted muslin wheel, and sanding disks.

curved bezel shears

Are you tired of struggling to cut curves? Buy a pair of curved shears to make cutting curves easier.

steel burnisher

This simple hand tool is great for smoothing the edges of metal shapes after cutting with shears. As you progress in metalworking, a burnisher will become a must-have tool for stone setting. In the meantime, you can use the back of a stainless steel spoon for eliminating sharp metal edges.

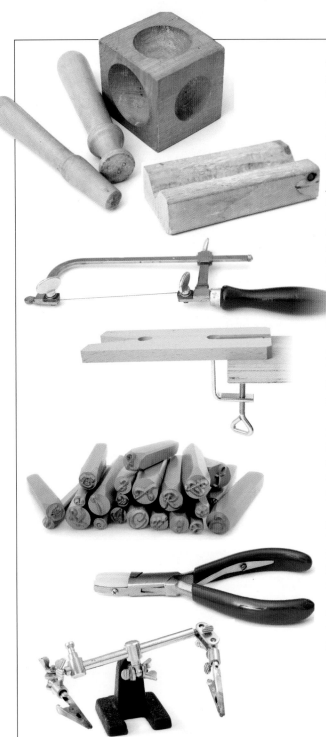

wood dapping block

A wood dapping set is an inexpensive way to get started dapping (doming) metal.

wood forming block

This block holds rings and bracelets as you form them around a mandrel. You can buy or make this tool (see p. 62).

jeweler's saw

A jeweler's saw is great for cutting thick metal and detailed lines. A 3" (76mm) or 4" (10.2cm) saw is a standard size and will work for all the projects in this book. A moderately priced saw has worked well for me. Check whether the saw you're buying has a tension screw; I like having one so I can adjust the blade tension. Don't forget to buy blade lubricant and blades with your saw. Use #2/0 blades for most of your work; for detailed work, consider a finer blade such as a #3/0. For cutting thick metal, use a #1 blade.

bench pin

This is basically a piece of wood with a V cut into it with a holder that clamps to your work table. The bench pin holds work in a good position for sawing.

metal stamps

Metal stamps are available in a plethora of choices, from different styles of alphabet letters to symbols of all kinds. Use metal stamps to create custom designs and a look of your own.

nylon-jaw pliers

These are flatnose pliers with wide nylon jaws. They are typically used for straightening wire, but they come in handy for other tasks such as bending ring shanks and manipulating metal sheet without marring it.

third hand

This adjustable tool acts as an extra hand to help hold pieces in position for soldering.

LUXURY TOOLS

Luxury tools are not essential but oh-so-delicious to have. These are the tools that make your workbench rock and are usually objects of envy. They make your life easier, but are typically not used every day.

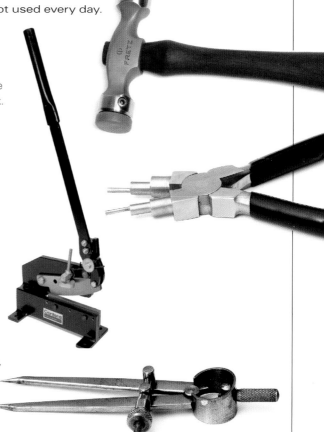

Fretz hammers
These are handcrafted, precision tools that are well-balanced and fit the hand perfectly. Until you have one in your hands, it is hard to know why you would ever pay a premium price for hammer. It is like driving a Rolls Royce; once you have driven one, it is hard to go back.

multi-looping pliers
You can do the same job with any roundnose pliers, but the advantage of using multi-looping pliers is the range of consistently sized loops that can be created. You won't need to mark your pliers or guesstimate anymore.

bench shear
This shear will cut a straight line through the thickest of metals. A good one cuts like butter. Most sheet metal is sold in a width of 6" (15.2cm). Buy a shear with a blade at least 8" (20.3cm) long so you will have to make only one cut to shear an entire piece.

dividers
Dividers look like a glorified compass from your school days. On metalsmith's dividers, however, both points are metal. Dividers will help you score straight lines for cutting metal. When used creatively, you can use dividers as a quick measuring tool to ensure the same measurement between pieces.

horn anvil
My anvil is about 8" (20.3cm) long and it has two horns: one is conical and the other has flatter surfaces. This tool is useful for working on small pieces such as rings. You'll be able to hammer different sizes of curves or corners into shapes depending on the position you use.

buy vintage!
Purchasing vintage tools is a good thing, even if they are rusty. (Rust usually can be removed.) My experience is that vintage tools are better than new ones: They were manufactured better, will more than likely last longer, and the steel is often higher quality than steel made today.

texturing hammer

Although you can create texture in a variety of less-fancy ways, texturing hammers are fun to have on your workbench. You'll find a variety of textures to choose from.

high-end ergonomic pliers

High-end ergonomic pliers are designed to be easier on your hands and wrists than standard pliers.

parallel pliers

These pliers act as a hand vise. They are great when you need to clamp something evenly. Parallel pliers clamp straight down instead of at an angle. I find most parallel pliers are too wide for my work, so I make the jaws narrower by grinding them with a grinding wheel on a lathe or on my flex shaft.

bracelet-bending pliers

Bracelet-bending pliers will make quick work of bending heavy-gauge wire or sheet metal for bracelets or a ring shank. Good bending pliers are adjustable so you can make bends at different angles.

rolling mill

Used to flatten sheet metal and make wire, this great tool is also used to transfer texture onto sheet metal. For example, you can use a rolling mill to transfer the impression of a leaf onto a piece of copper. You can make sheet metal thinner with a rolling mill—handy if you don't have the right gauge on hand.

metal dapping set

A metal dapping set is a step up from the wood set and will give you more options for doming metal.

OTHER TOOLS AND SUPPLIES

You may not need all these supplies for each project, but become familiar with them. Read over the techniques and tools called for in the project you want to make. If you choose to do the hot version of any project, you'll need the soldering setup listed below.

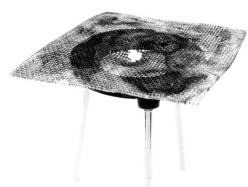

soldering setup

- butane torch and butane
- tripod with steel screen
- magnesia block or soldering block
- firesafe tweezers
- pickle (a commonly used brand is Sparex), electric crock pot, and rinse bowl with clean water
- copper tongs
- glass or metal quench bowl with clean water
- silver paste solder (hard, medium, and easy); copper paste solder
- flux (green flux and paste flux are commonly used types)

additional supplies

- patina solution (liver of sulfur or Black Max)
- adhesives (E6000, two-part epoxy, or New Glue)
- sandpaper (400-, 500-, and 600-grit)
- steel wool (#0000)

utility tools & supplies

Keep these items near your work bench for every project.

- metal ruler
- permanent markers: fine-tip and ultra-fine-tip Sharpies in black
- acetone and cotton pads: to remove Sharpie marks from metal surfaces
- paper
- cardstock
- pencil
- mechanical eraser
- gloves

The Basics: **techniques**

TOOLS
- roundnose pliers
- wire cutters (flush cutters preferred)
- chainnose pliers
- flatnose pliers

MATERIALS
- 50 2" (51mm) 24-gauge headpins
- beads

The wrong way to hold the pliers and wire.

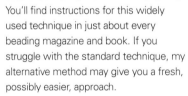

Making wire loops is a basic but essential skill in jewelry making. Practicing making loops will help you begin to understand how wire works.

MAKING SIMPLE LOOPS
You'll find instructions for this widely used technique in just about every beading magazine and book. If you struggle with the standard technique, my alternative method may give you a fresh, possibly easier, approach.

The key to my method is the hand position. It may feel awkward at first, but after you have practiced enough times, muscle memory will kick in and this will become second nature. Buy a 50-piece package of inexpensive headpins; when you have worked through them, you will have mastered this method.

Hold a pair of roundnose pliers in your dominant hand and a 24-gauge, 2"

(51mm) headpin (or piece of wire) in the other. When holding the pliers, turn your palm up so you are looking down at it, not at your knuckles. Your thumb should be pointing outward, away from your body **[A]**. Grasp the tip of the wire with your pliers as shown, making sure that the wire end is flush with the jaws **[B]**.

Where you grasp the wire on the jaw of the pliers will determine the size of your loop. The closer to the tip of the pliers you work, the smaller the loop will be. (Experiment with changing this position to see what I mean.)

Grasping the wire with the pliers, begin to roll toward your body **[C]**. This rolling action is important; by rolling, you are forcing the wire to form a perfect circle around the pliers **[D]**. Don't pull or twist the wire or you will create more of a hook or a corkscrew. Roll the pliers until the outside nose touches the inside of the wire **[E]**. Do not roll beyond this point or your wire will be misshapen.

If you rolled your pliers toward yourself, your knuckles should be up. Release the pliers and move the outside nose to the top of the loop without removing the inside nose from the loop **[F]**. Your loop may be closed at this point. If not, grasp the top of the loop and roll forward again to close. Release the pliers; move the outside nose to the inside of the loop **[G]**. Where the end of the loop meets the wire, grasp the wire and bend backward **[H]**. This will make your loop look like a lollipop **[I]**.

SIMPLE LOOPS WITH BEADS

When working with beads, slide the bead on a headpin and trim the wire approximately .63" (16mm) above the bead to make a 2mm loop **[J]**. (This length will vary depending on the size loop you are making.) After some practice, you will be able to easily estimate this length.

Hold the bead between your index finger and your thumb, with your middle finger stabilizing the headpin from below. Grasp the tip of the wire with the pliers as shown, making sure the wire is flush with the pliers. Again, ensure that you are holding the pliers with your palm up. Where you grasp the wire on the pliers determines the size of your loop **[K]**.

Grasping the wire firmly with the pliers, begin to roll toward your body **[L]**. Continue to roll the pliers until the outside nose touches the top of the bead **[M]**. Do not roll beyond this point or your bead may get damaged. If you have rolled your pliers towards yourself, your knuckles should be up.

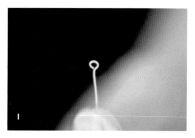

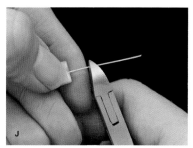

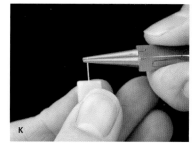

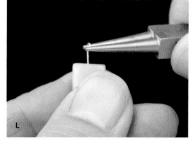

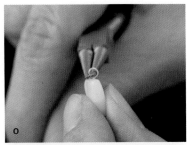

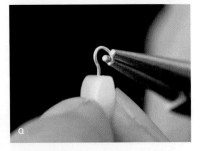

hand position

Always begin with the hand that is holding the roundnose pliers facing up so your thumb is pointing out like a hitchhiker and your palm is facing up. When you have completed your first turn, you should be looking at your knuckles as shown here.

Release the pliers and move the outside nose to the top of the loop without removing the inside nose from the loop. Grasp the top of the loop and roll it forward again to close the loop **[N]**.

Release the pliers and move the outside nose to the inside **[O]**. Where the end of the loop meets the wire, grasp the wire and bend backward. This will make your loop look like a lollipop **[P]**.

To make connections or add links, open the loop by pulling the end of the loop to one side **[Q]**, add the next link, and push the loop back into place. Do not pry the loop apart.

WRAPPED LOOPS WITH BEADS

A wrapped loop offers more security than the simple loop. This technique is an extension of my simple loop technique.

Use 24- or 26-gauge wire or headpins. Usually I use the heaviest wire that fits through the bead (unless the hole is ridiculously large). If the final product is going to take a lot of wear (as in a bracelet), use a heavier gauge such as 20 or 22. For earrings, where the loop will only be used to dangle a few beads, you can use a thin gauge like 24 or 26.

Start by sliding a bead onto a headpin. Hold the bead between your index finger and your thumb, with your middle finger stabilizing the headpin from below. Grasp the wire .25" (6.5mm) above the bead with your pliers, with the bead and wire underneath the pliers. Where you grasp the wire determines the loop size.

Grasp the wire with the pliers and begin to roll the wire toward your body **[A]**. Roll the pliers until the wire has made more than a half turn to create a T with the wires **[B, C]**. Do not roll beyond this point or you may damage your bead.

If you have gone too far, pull back on the pliers and reduce the size of the loop. Looking down at the wires, the cross wire should be on the bottom and to the side. Switch to chainnose or flatnose pliers (using your nondominant hand if you need to), and grasp the loop.

Holding the loop with chainnose pliers, use either a roundnose or another chain-nose pliers to grasp the extended wire **[D]** and pull it down toward the ground. It is a pulling motion, not a turning motion. Pull upward to begin wrapping around the base wire, and then pull down again **[E]**.

Continue until the stem is completely wrapped. When the wire begins to roll around your pliers, release the wire, turn your hand, and adjust your grasp. The number of wraps you make is up to you.

With small-head flush cutters or wire cutters, snip the excess wire close to the bead **[F]**. Tuck any excess wire by pinching the wire in with the tip of the chainnose pliers **[G]**. To straighten the loop, reinsert roundnose pliers and guide the loop back into shape **[H]**.

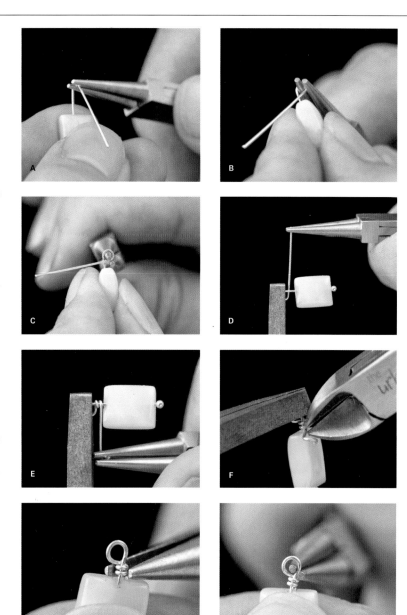

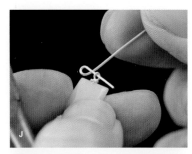

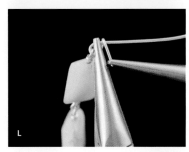

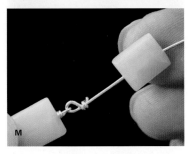

To create a different look, keep wrapping the wire onto the bead until the base wire is no longer exposed to create a spiral wire cap over the bead **[I]**.

→ TIP If the pliers are marring your work, dip the jaws in Tool Magic to coat them. If the coating diminishes the grip on the wire, remove the coating from one jaw of the pliers and use the coated side on the outside of the work to minimize marring.

WRAPPED LOOPS WITH BEAD LINKS

To create links, use 2" (51mm) of cut wire instead of a headpin. If you are using larger beads, you will need to cut more wire to accommodate the bead. You need at least .5" (13mm) of wire on each side of the bead. Make a wrapped loop at one end of the wire. Trim any excess wire. Slide a bead on the wire, make a wrapped loop with the remaining wire, and trim any excess wire.

To connect another bead link, turn another piece of wire until you reach the T step. Slide a completed unit onto the open loop you just created **[J]**. Using fine-tip chainnose pliers, grasp the new loop **[K]**. With another pair of pliers, pull the wire around the stem to wrap it **[L]**. Take care not to crush the link you are adding. Trim any excess wire. Tuck in the wire end using chainnose pliers. Slide another bead on the wire **[M]** and make a wrapped loop to complete the link. Repeat until you have enough links for your project.

CUTTING AND PIERCING METAL

TOOLS
- metal burnisher
- files
- bezel shears, straight
- dividers
- ruler
- Sharpie
- metal punch

MATERIALS
- 22- or 24-gauge sheet metal
- sandpaper, 400-grit

When you buy sheets of metal, they usually have sharp edges that can injure you. Before you start to work with them, burnish the edges: Hold a burnisher in your dominant hand with your thumb in the curve of the burnisher. Secure the sheet metal on the table by holding it down with the opposite hand, applying pressure on the metal with the burnisher and running the burnisher along the rough edge until it is smooth **[A]**.

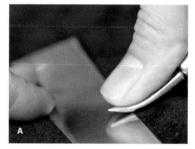

Repeat on each remaining edge, turn the metal over, and repeat on the back. You can use the bowl of a stainless steel spoon to burnish in the same way.

making straight cuts
If the metal already has straight edges, it's easy to mark other straight lines by using dividers. Score the sheet metal by applying a little pressure and dragging one point on the metal and the other point on the outer edge as a guide **[B]**. You can also use a metal ruler and an ultra-fine-tip Sharpie.

The tool you use to cut your metal is determined by the thickness (gauge) of the metal. I suggest using bezel shears on gauges up to the thickest sheet your hands can handle (or to the tolerance

rating of the shears). Beyond that, you will need to use a jeweler's saw (refer to The Basics: Sawing, p. 32).

Using bezel shears, cut the sheet metal as you would paper—a hard, heavy sheet of paper. When cutting, make long, smooth cuts instead of short cuts to prevent jagged edges. Open the shears and start a new cut before the tips of the shears close **[C]**. The cutting action will cause the edges to curl. To flatten curled

metal, place it on a bench block and hammer it flat with a rawhide or nylon mallet **[D]**. Take it easy; if you hammer too aggressively, you will mar the metal.

making rounded corners

To make rounded corners, first nip each corner at an angle with the shears **[E]**. File the nipped corners into a rounded shape **[F]**. To smooth the corners and edges, sand using 400- or 500-grit sandpaper until you feel no rough edges.

There are many tools you can use to pierce a hole in metal. A few oft-used methods are using a drill bit tightened in a pin vise, which takes some elbow grease, and using a flex shaft with high-speed drill bits. However, a few hand tools offer options; their limitations are the range of sizes and their reach. At some point, you may still want to use a simple pin vise or a flex shaft.

using a screw-down punch

Use this punch on soft metals like silver and copper up to 18-gauge. It makes holes in two sizes, usually 1.6mm and 2.3mm.

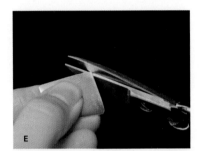

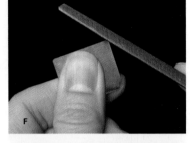

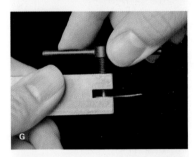

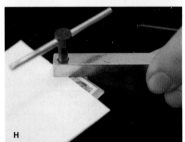

To use this type of punch, first mark a dot on the metal using a fine-tip Sharpie. Place the metal in the punch and begin to screw down, holding the metal to keep the mark in the right place. Continue to screw until you feel the bit loosen, and then begin to unscrew until the metal is released **[G]**. If you find the punch mars your metal, place a piece of cardstock (like a business card) between the metal and the punch as you unscrew **[H]**. If the hole punch leaves a burr, use the burnisher to smooth the metal or sand with sandpaper.

➔ TIP My two-hole punch is color-coded, so if yours looks like mine, remember: Black handle is for big, silver handle is for small. To hit your mark every time, turn the punch upside down, center the mark within the hole, and tighten the screw.

using a hand punch

Another great hand tool is the hand punch. These punches come in various sizes and can make holes in a variety of shapes. Use a hand punch as you would a paper punch **[I]**. Most can punch through soft metals up to a thickness of 24-gauge. These punches have a tendency to mar.

RIVETING: TUBE RIVETS

TOOLS
- burnisher
- screw-down punch
- Sharpie
- center punch
- riveting hammer
- bench block

MATERIALS
- 2x2mm or 2x3mm tubes
- 22–24-gauge sheet metal

To create a finished look for a cold connection and have the ability to add a gleam of contrasting metallic color, add a rivet through the holes using 2mm or 3mm copper or silver tubes. Mark the point for your connection. Using the large side of a screw-down punch, make a hole at each mark **[A]**.

Stand a tube on end on a bench block. Use a center punch with an end that tapers from a point to a diameter wider than the tube. Place the center punch directly on the tube **[B]** and gently tap the center punch with a riveting hammer **[C]**. Angle the punch in a circular motion until the tube is flared on one end **[D]**. Do not flare the tube too far; leave enough metal to work with on the other end.

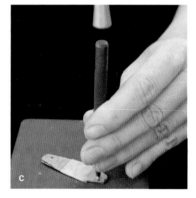

Flip the tube over, place the hole in the metal over the tube **[E]**, and flare the other end in the same way **[F]**. Work a little on each side, flipping the piece over and tapping so the tube is evenly flared on both sides of the metal. When both sides are evenly flared, finish the rivet by tapping directly on the rivet with a finishing punch or the face of the riveting hammer to flatten it **[G]**.

If your tube is long enough, you can layer several pieces of metal to create a connection with this technique: Simply

stack all the layers onto the tube after flaring one side and lock them into place by riveting the second side.

➡ **TIP** In hard-to-reach places like inside a dome, a finishing punch is especially handy for flattening and tightening the rivet after it's flared.

RIVETING: WIRE RIVETS

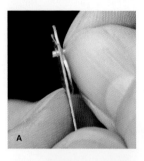
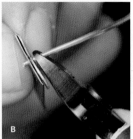
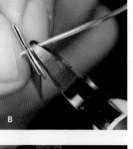
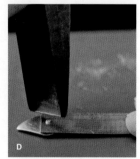
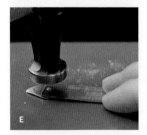
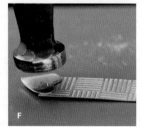
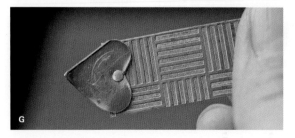

TOOLS
- burnisher
- screw-down punch
- ultra-flush wire cutters
- riveting hammer
- bench block
- Sharpie

MATERIALS
- 14-gauge sterling silver wire
- 22- or 24-gauge sheet metal

Wire rivets are a bit more challenging to make than tube rivets, but they offer a different look and are another solution for making a cold connection between two or more pieces of metal.

Mark the point of connection on each piece of metal. Using the small side of a screw-down punch, make a hole at each mark.

Using ultra-flush cutters, flush-cut the end of the 14-gauge wire. Slide the metal pieces onto the wire with 1mm of wire extending **[A]**. Flush-cut the other end of the wire **[B]**, again leaving 1mm of wire extending beyond the metal **[C]**.

Using the cross-peen face of a riveting hammer, tap the wire end to widen it into a rivet head that's wider than the hole **[D]**. Turn the pieces over and repeat until both heads match.

Finish the connection by tapping the wire flat on both sides of the metal with the face of the riveting hammer **[E, F]**. Work both sides by flipping the metal pieces back and forth and tapping to create flat, even rivet heads **[G]**.

METAL STAMPING

TOOLS
- 8 oz. utility hammer or brass-head mallet
- metal stamps
- bench block

MATERIALS
- 22–24-gauge sheet metal or metal shapes

Using economical 24-gauge copper sheet metal for practice, place the sheet on a bench block. Choose the metal stamp you want to use. Place the stamp on the sheet metal, holding firmly and low on the stamp, and rock the stamp gently back and forth until you feel the stamp in full contact with the metal.

Strike the stamp level as if you are hammering a nail **[A]**. One hard strike is preferred over several hits to prevent double impressions (unless you are using an especially large stamp, which will require more than one strike). Keep your eyes on the stamp at all times.

To stamp letters in a single straight line, draw a marker line slightly below the centerline of the disk with a ruler **[B]**. Place your line under the center by half the height of the letter stamp **[C]** (A line in the exact center will place your letters too high.)

→ **TIP** Always use a black marker. Colored marker is difficult to remove or hide if you stamp over the mark.

holding the hammer

Grip the hammer low on the handle

Don't choke up on the handle (hold it close to the head)

Grip the hammer with all your fingers; don't extend your thumb or index finger

more tips for stamping

Letter stamps are easier to punch than decorative stamps. The more intricate or larger the stamp, the more difficult it is to make a good impression.

When stamping words, consider the widths of all the letters as you determine the midpoint; the middle of the word "lime" is not between the "i" and the "m", but over the "m" ("m" and "e" are both wide letters).

Practice not only makes perfect, but will help you understand how hard to strike. Striking stamps too hard will warp the metal.

stamp buying guide

Today you have many options of metal stamps and stamp sets to choose from, which can be confusing and costly. Before buying, consider these factors and determine your needs.

Budget is at the top of many people's list. If you are not sure whether stamping is a technique you'll continue with, buy an inexpensive ($15–20) set of alphabet stamps to start. Some sets may have punctuation marks that can double as decorative stamps.

Letter stamps come in a wide variety of type styles. The least expensive have uppercase (capital) letters only. Generally, the more intricate the typeface, the more the set will cost. You may also want to compare how the capital letters look next to the lowercase letters.

The type of steel used not only affects the price but also the longevity of the stamp, and hard steel is most desirable. Zinc-based stamps are designed for working with leather and aren't suited for metalwork. Some stamps have been coated with zinc to prevent rusting. Although this seems practical, in time, the coating may transfer to your metal as it wears off and cause problems if you are soldering or enameling your pieces.

stamping ideas

Metal stamps can be used to "engrave" personal messages and create decorative impressions.

- Use letter and number stamps in a jumble to create an artistic look.
- The letters s, v, x, u, and o and numbers 8, 9, and 0 make terrific borders.
- You don't have to be limited to stamping a straight line. Create interest by adding curves.
- A center punch can be used for creating dots. Gently tap (not hammer) a center punch.
- If stamping a straight line seems impossible, stamp in an uneven line and it will look intentional.

the right hammer

Choosing the right hammer is mostly about how comfortable it feels in your hand. If a hammer is too heavy for you, it is not a safe choice, and a hammer that is too light will make the work harder than it needs to be. An 8–16-oz. household hammer is ideal for stamping metal. Your hammer does not have to be fancy or expensive to do the job. Chasing hammers and jeweler's hammers used to forge wire and metal should not be used, or you will mar their faces.

Some metalworkers prefer to use a brass hammer to strike stamps because brass is softer than steel; in general, this is only critical if you're using expensive chasing tools or stamps. For our purposes, either steel or brass is fine.

Heavy hammers are great for intricate and large stamps. They make your work a lot easier, allowing you to do the job in one blow. But be very careful using heavy hammers: Your wrist will tire sooner and reduce accuracy.

A preference for a standard handle vs. a short handle is purely up to the user. Whichever one makes you most comfortable is the one you should choose.

Always keep your fingers out of the hammer's way and pay attention to what you are hammering to avoid hitting them.

ADDING COLOR

In the old days, if you said metal had patina, you meant that it had been exposed to the elements and had developed some lovely colors or other signs of age. To get an aged or even ancient look on metal, you could leave the metal out in the open and wait—but who has time for that? Today you can find many products that create similar looks in minutes instead of months or years. A few things to remember when using patina products: Not all are permanent, and because patina also occurs naturally and continuously, the metal will continue to change color.

Sharpie
Using a black Sharpie is the fastest and easiest way to add color in after you've stamped metal or textured it. This is a semi-permanent effect and can wear off over time.

Black Max
This is an acid-based liquid that works on contact. Use this product with caution; wear gloves and work on a protected surface. Apply Black Max to metal with a cotton swab. Neutralize by washing with water. Use a polishing pad, sandpaper, or steel wool to remove excess color **[A]**. For safe storage of Black Max, place the bottle inside of another container and store it away from metal tools.

liver of sulfur (LOS)
This is a mixture of potassium sulfide that comes in rock, liquid, or gel form. The rock and gel forms must be diluted with water to use. (Using warm water will help LOS work faster.)

Although LOS is easy to use, it's a little unpredictable, so duplicating a color or effect is not so easy. LOS responds differently to various factors such as distilled water vs. well water, using a foam cup vs. a glass container, and temperature of the water. If the strong smell of hardboiled eggs bothers you, I suggest applying LOS outdoors. Solution made from the rock form can be stored for future use if you place it in an airtight jar and store in a dark place; it should last about 2 months. The gel form can be stored for a few days at most.

To use, dilute some LOS in a small bowl or jar with warm water, and place your metal pieces in the solution **[B]**. Watch for changes, remove when the metal is the desired color, and rinse in water **[C]**. Remove excess color and polish the high points with a polishing pad, sandpaper, or steel wool.

heat patina on copper
Experiment with applying heat from a torch to change the color of copper. Lightly heat the piece for a few seconds. Remove the flame and watch the color develop as the metal cools. Repeat if you want to intensify the color. You can get some beautiful reds with this method.

Gilders paste
This is a semipermanent, beeswax-based product that comes in a rainbow of colors. Using your fingers, you can add a little or a lot of color to metal **[D]**. After the paste dries, buff the piece lightly with a paper towel or steel wool. You can use mineral spirits to remove dried paste if necessary.

ANNEALING AND SOLDERING

annealing

In annealing, you soften metal by heating it to make it more malleable. This process may be applied to sheet metal or wire as many times as needed as the metal becomes work-hardened. To anneal sheet metal or wire, place it on a mesh screen on a tripod and heat it with the butane torch flame until the metal glows rosy (but not red). Pick it up with tweezers, quench, and pickle it before using. Depending on the type of metal and size, you may need the larger flame of a jumbo butane torch for successful annealing. You can anneal copper, silver, brass, or nickel this way.

How can you tell if metal has been annealed properly? Bend it. It should bend easily and not spring back.

soldering

I use an easy-to-operate handheld butane torch to create all the projects. In the hot version of each project, I explain the detailed soldering steps you'll need to follow. These pages give a general introduction to soldering, including safety and troubleshooting tips.

Soldering is the process of joining two pieces of metal together by melting solder (an alloy) to fill the join. In essence, soldering is like an adhesive for metal. Solder is available in several forms: wire, sheet, and paste. With wire and sheet solder, you must first apply flux to the components to help the solder flow and minimize firescale or oxidation. Flux is built into paste solder, simplifying the preparation a bit.

The different forms of solder have different advantages, but usually it comes down to simple preference. I find paste solder quite easy to apply, so I use it most often. Paste solder use is what's shown throughout this book.

Solder also comes in many types rated by melting point, including hard (high melting point), medium, easy, and extra-easy (low melting point). This is important if you are making a project that has multiple joins: Start with the hardest solder for the first join and work your way through solder with progressively lower melting points. If you use the solder with the same melting point throughout the process, you run the

risk of reopening previous solder joins as you heat the piece up to the same temperature. (As you get better at flame control, you can avoid this.)

For example, in making a ring, first create the bezel (first join, hard solder), solder the bezel to the back plate (second join, medium solder), and then solder the back plate to the ring shank (third join, easy solder). By stepping down with every join, you ensure that the previous solder join stays closed.

Rules to silver soldering are similar to the principles of gluing:

1. The join must be clean. As in gluing, if there are oils or impurities present, the solder won't stick. To clean the metal, file, sand, or pickle it (the easiest method is pickling—immersing it in a warm bath of acidic solution).

2. The two pieces to be joined must be flush. Simply make the pieces meet perfectly with attention to filing and sanding smooth. You must not be able to see light through the join.

3. Solder follows heat. You must heat the metal evenly so the solder flows properly. If you heat unevenly, the solder will flow to the hottest part and the solder will not join the pieces fully, if at all.

torch safety

1. Tie your hair back; wear cotton clothing and closed-toe shoes; remove long and dangling jewelry.

2. Always work in a well-ventilated area. Metalwork and soldering involve gases and fumes.

3. Work over your workbench, not over your lap.

4. Identify your tools by looking at them before you pick them up. As beaders, we have a tendency to use the tool that is closest to us. When using heat, it's important to avoid harming your tools or yourself.

5. Keep a fire extinguisher, first aid kit, and baking soda nearby. Use baking soda to neutralize any pickle that drips or spills.

6. Use the torch in your nondominant hand and any other tool in your dominant hand. Keeping a tool in one hand can help prevent you from touching hot metal.

7. When quenching hot metals (dipping them in water to cool them), always quench the entire piece, not just the part you are heating.

8. Never point the torch at anything other than what you are working on.

9. Keep your soldering area clear of flammable items like paper and draperies.

10. If you're sharing studio space, be aware of your workspace and the workspace of people around you.

troubleshooting

If your metal is melting before the solder flows or the solder does not take, here are a few things you should consider:
1. The piece is not being heated evenly (silver soldering).

2. The join is dirty. Try pickling the piece and starting over.

3. There is not enough heat. Perhaps the piece you are soldering is too heavy and the torch you are using does not provide enough heat for the solder to flow.

terms to learn

Firescale is oxidation that forms on the surface of your metal as result of being exposed to the flame. To remove it, you can use sandpaper or simply place it in warm pickle solution.

Flow is the point when solder reaches its melting point and turns molten. The solder looks like liquid silver. Being able to see solder flow and recognizing the point at which to stop heating is key to making the perfect join.

Pickle is an acid used to remove firescale (oxides) and impurities on the surface of silver, gold, copper, and brass caused by heating. Traditionally, pickle is made of sulfuric acid, but sodium bisulfate is more commonly used today. When a

piece refuses to solder, most of the time it's because the metal or the solder is dirty. The easiest way to assess the problem is to pickle it; if that doesn't work, you have a different problem. You can pickle a metal piece as many times as needed as you are working on it.

some rules for pickle

1. The only metals that should go into pickle are silver, gold, copper, and brass. Never put ferrous metal (such as steel pliers) in pickle.

2. Never put hot metal in pickle; this may cause the acid to splash back at you. It can damage fabric, skin, and eyes.

3. Never heat pickle on the stove or in the microwave; use a warming pot (a small electric crock pot works great).

4. Use pickle warm or hot for fast results. It can be used cold; it just takes longer.

5. Keep the pickle pot covered to prevent water from evaporating and keep you from breathing fumes. If the solution dries up, just add more distilled water.

6. Dispose of pickle properly. It should be neutralized before disposal. Refer to the MSDS that comes with it or talk with your local hazardous waste disposal team.

SAWING

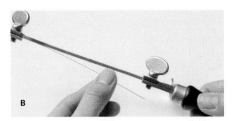

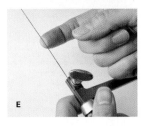
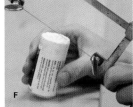

Don't be afraid of using a jeweler's saw. I find sawing to be meditative and relaxing. Sawing is useful when you need to cut shapes out of metal that are a little more complicated than your shears can handle.

loading the saw

Loosen the top and bottom screws slightly. Place the saw blade in the top of the frame with the teeth facing down, so that when you are holding the saw up, the blade looks like a pine tree **[A]**. Tighten the top screw.

If necessary, adjust the length of the frame to accommodate the length of the blade **[B]**. You want about .25–.50" (6.5–13mm) of blade clamped in the bottom of the frame. Place the saw as shown against a table, lean into the handle, and tighten the lower screw against the blade to create tension **[C]**. You can also tighten the blade by placing the saw on the table as shown, pulling down on the handle, and tightening the back screw **[D]**. Check the tension of the blade by flicking it with your finger **[E]**. It should make a "ping" sound; it should not be high pitched (too tight) or dull sounding (too loose) or it will break easily while sawing. Before you start sawing, lubricate the blade by gently moving the blade up and down over some paraffin or blade lubricant **[F]**.

pin vise, rotary tool, or flex shaft?

I mentioned earlier that you have many options when it comes to piercing holes in metal, including a simple hand punch or screw-down punch. If you are on a budget and space is limited, a pin vise is a great tool to have on hand, but not all pin vises are created equal. My favorite has a wood handle that spins. This spinning action allows you to apply downward pressure while you turn the vise with your fingers. It also comes with four collets, which tighten to grip the bit. Chances are one of the collets will fit any bit you own.

Even if you are a relative newcomer to jewelry making, you may already own a handheld rotary tool (Dremel is a recognized brand). If this is the case, use what you have—at least until you grow out of it or can afford a flex shaft. Before

you start working with the rotary tool, look through the bits and pieces that came with it and ensure that you have the right size of collets to hold the bits you work with; you may need to buy collets small enough to handle jewelry-making bits. You can attach a flex-shaft-like handpiece to a rotary tool, which makes it a little less cumbersome to hold and use.

A flex shaft is a jewelry maker's best friend, and it's considered standard equipment on every pro jeweler's bench. This is a great tool that will make your life easier. Its motor is separate from the "business end," the handpiece; the motor hangs from a hook above the work surface. The handpiece is easy to hold and control. A flex shaft can be used for everything from piercing to polishing.

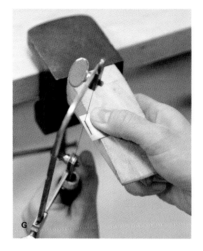

Sawing action

Posture is a very important part of sawing correctly. Sit with the bench pin just below chest height, plant your feet flat on the floor and apart with the bench pin between your legs, and relax your shoulders. Put the metal flat on the bench pin, hold the saw loosely, and move it straight up and down against the metal. If the saw resists, do not force it or you will break your blade.

→ TIP If you break a blade, clear the clamp of debris and shorten the saw's throat length to fit the shorter blade.

To turn a corner, saw in place while gently turning the saw **[G]** until you have made the full turn **[H]**. Continue sawing forward after you make the turn (you may want to reposition the metal at this point).

To create a cutout in the middle of a piece, begin by piercing a hole in the metal: First, draw the design with a Sharpie. In the middle of the design, where there will be a cutout, punch a hole either with a hole punch or a pin vise **[I]**. Open the bottom clamp of the saw to release the blade, slide the metal onto the blade with the outlined design face up, and tighten the blade in the clamp **[J]**. Hold the metal piece between the V of the bench pin, and begin to saw.

using patterns

To create patterns of your own for sawing out of metal, use a stencil, cut a pattern from paper, use a rubber stamp, or draw freehand on the metal with a Sharpie. If you make a pattern from paper or trace a template from this book, use rubber cement to adhere the paper to the metal. You don't need to cut out the shape first—just saw right through the paper and peel it off after you finish sawing.

TEXTURING

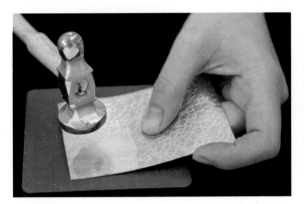 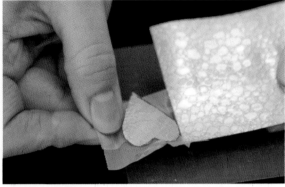

The easiest way to add texture to your work is to buy textured metal sheet instead of plain sheet, but it's fairly easy to create your own textures too.

One way is to purchase brass texture sheets and transfer the texture onto plain metal. First, cut your finished shape out of metal. Secure the plain metal to the textured side of the texture sheet with clear packaging tape, and place this sandwich on a bench block with the plain metal on top. With the wide face of a chasing hammer, gently strike the plain metal evenly **[A]**. Don't strike too hard in any one place or you'll distort the metal. Separate the pieces and remove the tape **[B]**. The shape will have a shallow texture.

If you want a deeper impression, texture the metal first using greater force, and then cut it to shape. Texturing will work-harden the metal; you may need to anneal it to soften the metal before you cut or form it (refer to p. 30).

other texturing options

Letter stamps: Don't overlook your letter stamp set for a source of interesting textures. Repeat letters, numbers, and punctuation marks to make playful patterns.

Chasing hammer: Use the ball-peen side to create a hammered look, or use the edge to create a hash-mark texture.

Texture hammers: You can buy hammers with readymade textures; some have interchangeable faces. Using them is simple and fun: Place the metal on a bench block and hammer to your heart's content.

Sandpaper: Sanding the metal with sandpaper will create a variety of different looks; 400-grit will produce a matte finish, 150-grit creates a sandblasted look, and 150-grit used in two directions produces a diamond pattern. You can also try sanding in a circular motion.

Rolling mill: Place the metal between a textured piece and a light piece of cardstock and roll through.

FILING AND SANDING

The difference between a good jeweler and a great jeweler is in the finishing. If you take the time to properly finish a piece, you'll have a much better end result. Finishing is tedious work, but the rewards are worth the effort.

File and sand your metal to remove anything that's marring the surface, such as hammer or pliers marks.

Filing

Filing is the first step in finishing. If your piece needs a lot of filing, start with a coarse (#2) file. This file will remove a lot of metal, so be careful not to damage your piece. As you get close to the finished shape or line you want, switch to a fine-grit needle file. Match the shape of the file to the shape of the metal you are filing.

To file, simply file back and forth as you would to shape your fingernails. Many people believe that you should only file in one direction (away from you), because that is the motion that removes metal, but I prefer to go both ways. If you are trying to file a straight edge, take care to file straight. Place the piece you are filing against your workbench or bench pin for resistance. This will allow the file to be more effective.

If you are one of the people who look at "file" as a four-letter word, opt for a coarse-grit sandpaper (100- or 150-grit), which will make fast work of removing metal.

Sanding

Wet/dry sandpaper found at the hardware store, emery boards, or sanding blocks can all be used for sanding. If you have a hard time finding sandpaper (especially the super-fine grits), try your local auto body or guitar store. Sanding is the next step after filing has shaped the metal as you want it

If you are sanding a straight edge or surface of the metal, place the sandpaper on a flat surface and rub the metal against the sandpaper in either a circular motion or a figure-8 pattern.

For a high-polish finish, sand using a progression of grits from coarse to fine after all of the connections are made: Beginning with 400-grit sandpaper, sand in one direction until all of the surface scratches are even. Turn the piece 90 degrees and sand with the next-finest grit until all the marks from the previous grit are removed and you have progressed to at least 600-grit. When you're finished sanding, you can move to final polishing.

GLUING

Although it's always preferable to use a hot or cold connection in metalwork, you may choose use glue for certain tasks from time to time. Use powerful glue designed for adhering nonporous materials. I always use the strongest available for the project at hand.

At the top of my list is two-part epoxy. This is the stuff they use to put together the body of a Corvette. It should hold a few pieces of metal together, right? The challenge to epoxy is the mixture. If you do not mix it perfectly in the right proportions, it will not hold. Epoxy is also really goopy, so I reserve it for larger projects.

For small projects, I use New Glue, a super-strong cyanoacrylate glue from Eurotool. New Glue is very watery and has a tendency to run, so use it sparingly. Use a stick pin to apply it to small spaces.

E6000 is a great general-use adhesive. It's perfect for use with large items and does not require mixing. Like epoxy, E6000 is goopy, which makes it challenging to use on small projects.

Even if the package says that an adhesive will set in just a few minutes, allow a 24-hour curing time for best results.

POLISHING

There are many polishing options. The following list is ordered from the least expensive to most expensive ways to polish. Polishing should be done after you've removed all deep scratches and marks by filing and sanding.

To **polish by hand**, buff the piece with a polishing pad or polishing cloth.

A **rotary tumbler** has a motor and a belt that rotates a barrel with stainless steel shot inside. This motion of the shot against the metal piece burnishes and polishes the metal while you do

something else **[A]**. An inexpensive rock tumbler will work well for awhile, but the more you tumble, the more likely you will need to invest in a good-quality tumbler designed for jewelry making.

→ **TIP** Tumbling is also a great way to remove tarnish from old silver beads. String the beads together before tumbling.

To tumble, place your pieces in the barrel with stainless steel shot (jeweler's mix), water, and several drops of burnishing solution or liquid dish soap. Tumbling time can be anywhere from 15 minutes to an hour or more. Most beads and gemstones can handle tumbling, but do not tumble pieces with soft or porous materials, such as pearls, turquoise, or opal.

A **flex shaft or rotary tool** with a mounted muslin wheel and Tripoli or jewelers rouge (polish) will give you the most professional look without the expense of a buffing wheel on a lathe.

To polish metal, spin a mounted muslin wheel lightly on a bar of polishing compound until there is a fair amount of polish on the wheel. Press the spinning wheel on the metal surface and edges **[B]**. Continue until you have touched all surfaces with the wheel and polish. Don't be afraid to be aggressive.

As you polish, the surface will turn black from the polish residue. This will be washed off and can be ignored for now. Concentrate on touching every surface that you want to be polished. Be careful not to overheat the metal (you'll burn your fingers). Wash under running water with a toothbrush and a drop of dish soap to remove any polish residue. If the surface doesn't have a mirror shine, repeat the polishing.

Using a **buffing wheel on a bench lathe** is the most professional way to polish. This large wheel will make quick to work of polishing and is less messy. Prep your metal as with a flex shaft: Apply polishing compound to the buff, and engage the metal against the spinning wheel lightly until all surfaces are polished. Clean the metal with soapy water.

The Projects
hot & cold pairs

TUBE RIVETS

SOLDERED TUBE

Memento pendants

This mini-book project will teach you how to cut metal with shears and round the sharp corners. If your hands aren't super-strong (yet!), use 26-gauge copper. Otherwise, you may use any type of metal to create a look of your own, but practice with copper before cutting sterling silver.

Both versions, cold and hot, will start to refine your metal skills because they require accuracy. The cold project introduces tube rivets. You'll make a front and back cover plus an inside page that can include an image. The hot project introduces piercing and soldering: You will cut copper tubing and solder it closed to bind the book.

TOOLS & SUPPLIES

- bezel shears, straight
- burnisher
- files
- chainnose pliers
- rawhide or nylon-head mallet
- bench block
- screw-down punch
- dividers
- metal alphabet stamps or decorative stamps
- Sharpie
- acetone
- cotton pad
- acrylic glaze
- liver of sulfur or Black Max
- polishing pads
- sandpaper

MATERIALS

- 24- or 26-gauge copper sheet, 1x3" (25.5x76mm)
- 2x3mm silver tubes, 4
- laser-printed image, .75"x.75" (19x19mm)
- 19- or 20-gauge 6mm OD jump rings, 2

Burnish all edges of the sheet metal before you begin working (refer to The Basics: Cutting and Piercing Metal, p. 23). Cut three squares of metal of the same size; these will be the front and back cover and a single page for your book. (Cut more if desired. You may need to use larger jump rings if you add a lot of pages.) If you don't have dividers, measure your squares carefully using a metal ruler or graph paper and mark them on the metal.

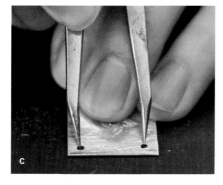

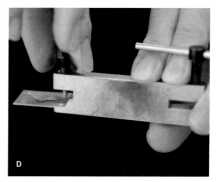

To use dividers, open the tool to 1" (25.5mm) or the desired width; place one point on the metal and the other on the outside edge. Press firmly while dragging the dividers along the metal to create a score line **[A]**.

Cut along the line with bezel shears, making long cuts. Score and cut the remaining side of the square. With the rawhide or nylon-head mallet, flatten the pieces on the bench block **[B]**.

Mark two holes, placing each hole .13" (3mm) from the top edge and .13" from each side edge of what will be the book cover. Dividers make marking easy **[C]**.

Punch the holes using the larger screw of the screw-down punch **[D]**.

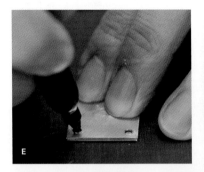 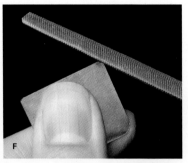 

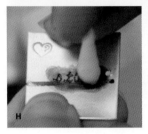  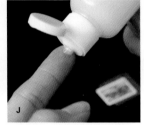 

Use this first piece as a guide to mark two holes for the back cover with a Sharpie **[E]**. Punch the holes in the back cover.

With bezel shears, snip each corner of each square at an angle and use a file to create rounded corners **[F]**. Sand as needed with a progression of sandpaper to remove all rough edges so the pendant is comfortable when worn.

Stamp a custom design or message onto the cover (refer to The Basics: Metal Stamping, p. 27) **[G]**. I drew a marker line to help me position the letter stamps. Remove any pen marks with acetone and a cotton swab or pad **[H]**. Add patina to the stamped areas of the cover (refer the Basics: Adding Color, p. 29).

Add tube rivets to the holes you made in the front cover to create a finished look (refer to The Basics: Tube Rivets, p. 25) **[I]**.

Use the cover as a guide to mark holes on the top corners of the interior page with a pencil. Punch the hole using the small screw of the screw-down punch.

For the image page, use any laser-printed image that is at least 20% smaller than the metal page and an acrylic-based glaze.

→ TIP Inkjet prints will not work because the glaze will cause the ink to run. If you do not have a laser printer, your local photo or copy shop can reduce images and make prints for you.

Using your fingertips, apply glaze to the back of the image and adhere it to the metal page **[J]**. Apply another thin layer over the image and the metal to seal **[K]**. Allow the glaze to dry, add another layer to the top, and let dry completely.

→ TIP Apply glaze in thin layers for the best results.

To assemble, attach the squares with jump rings through the corner holes. Hang on a chain if desired.

TOOLS & SUPPLIES
- bezel shears, straight
- burnisher
- files
- rawhide or nylon-head mallet
- bench block
- screw-down punch
- chainnose pliers
- bench saw
- scrap wood
- dividers
- metal alphabet stamps or decorative stamps
- pin vise
- .5mm twist drill bit
- tube-cutting pliers (optional)
- flex shaft (optional)
- brass-bristle brush (optional)
- bench knife or butter knife
- 2/0 saw blades
- 500-grit sandpaper
- copper paste solder
- acrylic glaze
- soldering setup
- third hand
- liver of sulfur or Black Max
- polishing pads

MATERIALS
- 24- or 26-gauge silver, 3x1" (76x25.5mm)
- copper tubing,.38" (9.5mm) or .88" (22mm)

→ **TIP Find copper tubing in the plumbing department of your local hardware store. Small, independently owned stores usually sell tubing by the foot.**

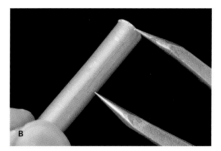

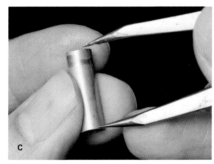

Referring to the instructions for the cold-connected version, cut three 1" (25.5mm) squares from silver sheet and round the corners of each square.

Determine the length you want for the copper tube binding of your book (mine was .88"/22mm) **[A]**. Transfer this size to the tubing using dividers or a ruler **[B]**. Saw the tubing to length (refer to p. 42).

Double check the length of the tube with the dividers or a ruler **[C]**. Transfer the size by marking two dots on one edge of each metal square. Draw a straight line between the marks with a straight edge **[D]**.

Stamp custom messages and designs on each square as desired (refer to Basics: Metal Stamping, p. 27).

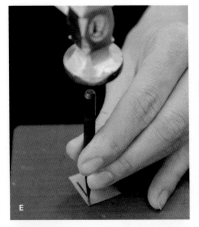

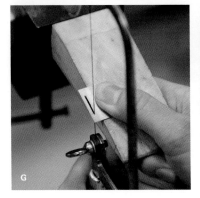

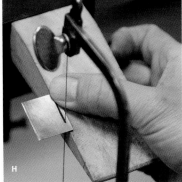

Here are two methods for sawing the tube. Remember to lubricate your blade and make sure you have the right tension.

Method #1
Using tube-cutting pliers, clamp the tube with the mark between the slit of the pliers. Hold the pliers with the tube in front of you, firmly placed against your work bench. Saw back and forth between the slit of the pliers until you have cut through the tube.

Method #2
Clamp the tube firmly in a vise, but not so tightly that it warps the tube. Saw until you cut through the tube. You can also use a bench pin or tape the tube so the part you want to cut hangs off the edge of your work bench.

Gently tap a starter divot at one end of the line with a center punch and chasing hammer on a bench block **[E]**. Using a pin vise and a .5mm drill bit, pierce a small hole. This will serve as an entry point for the saw blade **[F]**.

➜ TIP I drill over a piece of scrap wood to eliminate drill holes in my bench.

Release the bottom of the saw blade. Slip the drilled metal into the blade with the mark facing up. Slide the metal to the top of the saw blade to help you

tighten the blade into place without resistance (refer to The Basics: Sawing, p. 32).

Slide the metal to the bottom of the saw, place it on the bench pin, and begin to saw the length of your mark **[G]**. This opening will not be wide enough for the copper tubing; you will need to widen the opening by turning the blade and making another cut.

Move the blade straight up and down in place while slowly turning the saw until you are 180 degrees from the start. Flip the metal and begin to saw back to the starting point **[H]**. If this opening is still not wide enough for your tubing, enlarge it by filing.

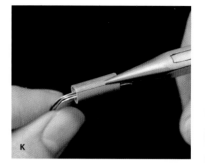

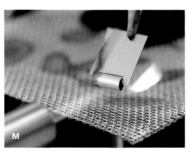

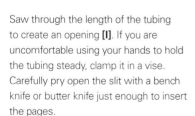

Saw through the length of the tubing to create an opening **[I]**. If you are uncomfortable using your hands to hold the tubing steady, clamp it in a vise. Carefully pry open the slit with a bench knife or butter knife just enough to insert the pages.

Slide the pages onto the tubing **[J]**. Use chainnose pliers to close the tubing so the edges align **[K, L]**.

Place a few drops of copper solder paste along the inside edge. Place the entire book on a tripod with mesh or on a soldering block. You can clamp the book in a third hand, if desired.

Heat the copper tubing. You may see flames from the inside of the tube, but don't worry; this is just flux burning off **[M]**. Continue to heat until you see solder flow through the join **[N]**. Quench it in cool water, and place it into warm pickle solution.

→ TIP Copper solder takes longer to set than silver solder.

When the firescale has disappeared (the copper should look rosy), remove the book from the pickle with copper tongs, rinse it in water, and dry it.

With a brass brush in a rotary tool or a flex shaft, polish all the pages and tubing. If there is excess solder on the seam, use 500-grit sandpaper to remove.

Sand the entire tube to create an even surface.

Add a patina to add definition to the stampings (refer to The Basics: Adding Color, p. 29).

WIRE
BINDING

SOLDERED
JUMP RING

Kisses pendants

Using wire to bind metal shapes together is a great way to make connections. Although the cold version of this project may look easy, the challenge is keeping your wires straight. You may be tempted to use a heavier wire to reduce breakage, but don't: Heavy-gauge wire is harder to work with. Practice with scrap material and take your time. Getting good at binding becomes easier the more you work with wire. You'll get to know how it likes to move and when it's getting overworked.

The hot version introduces hammering and forging metal. You will likely need to solder the pieces in more than one step, which will challenge your skills.

TOOLS & SUPPLIES
- bezel shears, straight
- bezel shears, curved
- scissors
- burnisher (optional)
- files
- rawhide or nylon-head mallet
- bench block
- screw-down punch
- nylon-jaw pliers
- wire cutters
- chainnose or flatnose pliers
- mini stepped mandrel or roundnose pliers
- Sharpie
- acetone
- cotton pad or swab
- sandpaper (optional)
- bench knife or butter knife
- steel wool or polishing pad

MATERIALS
- 24-gauge textured copper, 3x3" (76x76mm)
- 22-gauge copper or plated wire, 12" (30.5cm)

Cut two matching hearts about 1" (25.5mm) wide from your metal. Mark dots for two holes in a straight line; one near the V of the shoulders and one near the point. Pierce a hole at each dot using the small bit of the screw-down punch **[A, B]**. Use the first heart as a template to mark dots on the second heart. This will help line up your holes correctly.

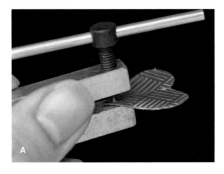

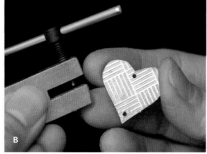

drawing good hearts
You can use my pattern or design your own: Fold a scrap of paper in half, draw half a heart about .5" (13mm) wide, and cut it out. Open the heart and trace it onto the metal.

TEMPLATE

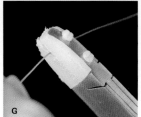

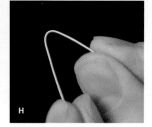

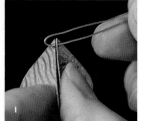

Create a fold along the centerline of the heart using the edge of a bench block or anvil and a chasing hammer: Place half of the heart (texture side down) on the block with the centerline along the edge. Hold the heart firmly with one hand and hammer directly on the edge of the anvil to begin to form a line [C].

As a line starts to form, turn the hammer so it faces the edge of the anvil. Strike to continue folding the heart [D, E]. It may help your leverage to move the block to the edge of your workbench or place it on top of a telephone book or board [F]. Use a needle file and sandpaper to smooth any sharp edges (refer to The Basics: Filing and Sanding, p. 35).

Repeat to make a fold in the second heart. Apply patina to both pieces as desired. I applied a torch patina to my heart (refer to The Basics: Adding Color, p. 29) and removed the patina from the high points with steel wool or a polishing pad.

Cut 12" (30.5cm) of copper or copper-plated 22-gauge wire. Straighten the wire by firmly holding it in one hand and pulling it through nylon-jaw pliers [G]. If you don't have nylon-jaw pliers, put plastic bandages on your index finger and thumb (or

wear gloves) and pull the wire between your fingers.

Bend the wire in half [H]. Match up the holes of the two hearts. Insert one end of the wire through the bottom holes of each heart, stopping at the bend [I]. Shift the wire so each

end extends toward the shoulders, with one piece on each side of the double heart. Insert one end through the top hole of each heart [J]. Insert the other end through the same hole in the opposite direction.

→ TIP As you work, continue to straighten the wire to keep the work neat.

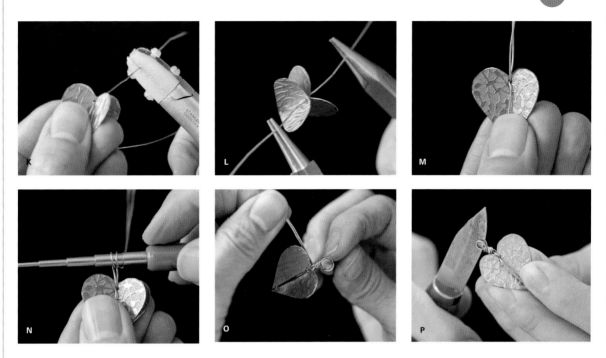

Using nylon-jaw pliers, pull the wire tightly through the hole [K]. Using two pairs of pliers, grasp each wire end and pull to bring the hearts tightly together [L]. Bring the wire ends together and fold them up [M].

Using a mini step mandrel or roundnose pliers, make a wrapped loop with both wire ends [N]. Wrap the wire around the stem [O]. Trim any excess wire.

Use a bench knife or butter knife to separate the loops of the bail [P].

TOOLS AND SUPPLIES

- bezel shears, straight
- bezel shears, curved (optional)
- burnisher
- files
- rawhide or nylon-head mallet
- bench block
- Sharpie
- anvil (optional)
- flatnose pliers
- soldering setup with magnesia block
- copper paste solder
- steel U-pins

MATERIALS

- 24-gauge textured copper, 3x3" (76x76mm)
- 6–7mm OD copper jump ring

 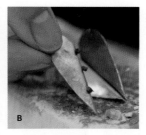 

Cut three matching hearts about 1" (25.5mm) wide from textured metal.

Hammer each heart on the edge of a bench block to create matching folds. (Refer to the cold version of this project.)

→ **TIP** Bend steel wire to make your own U-pins.

Place a magnesia block on top of a piece of steel screen on a tripod. Set two hearts on the block and secure them with U-pins to keep them from moving while soldering **[A]**. Place several dabs of paste solder along the fold of the third heart **[B]**. Secure as shown, adjusting the U-pins as needed. It is OK if the

edges do not touch. The key to make sure that all three pieces are touching at the center folds, where the pieces will join.

Because you are using one solder join to attach multiple pieces, you will need to heat all the pieces evenly to ensure that solder flows evenly. (If the solder does not flow evenly, solder only two pieces first instead of all three.) Keep the torch moving from side to side. Flame or smoke will appear as the flux burns off; this is normal **[C]**. Keep the application of heat steady until the solder flows **[D]**. If you stop midstream, the flux may burn off without the solder flowing properly.

It will be difficult to see the solder flow, but you should see movement in the metal pieces (almost like a sinking action). When you notice this, turn off the torch. Allow a moment for the solder to set before carefully removing the assembly from the block using firesafe tweezers. Quench in cool water. If only two pieces joined, pickle all the pieces, set them up again, apply more solder, and heat again.

setup option
Prop the pieces upright: You'll be able to heat them from all angles, helping create an even flow of solder.

If the sides of the pieces are not tight against each other, pinch them together with a pair of flatnose pliers **[E]**. File all the edges so they are even **[F]**. Sand as needed.

To create a bail, solder a jump ring onto the pendant: Secure the piece on the magnesia block with U-pins so it stays upright. Place a 3mm dab of paste solder between the shoulders of the hearts **[G]**. (This is a lot of solder, but because this point will be stressed, it's good to use more rather than less.)

Begin heating the paste solder with one hand while holding a jump ring in firesafe tweezers with the other hand. Place the seam of the jump ring toward the pendant **[H]**. Aim the flame a bit below the jump ring so the jump ring gets warm but not too hot. When the solder begins to flow, lower the jump ring to the solder point until the solder attaches to the ring **[I, J]**.

Quench the pendant **[K]** and place it in the pickle **[L]**. Rinse and dry it. Use steel wool, a brass-bristle brush, or a buffing wheel in a flex shaft to clean the surface and restore the bright copper color (refer to The Basics: Polishing, p. 36). Add patina if desired (refer to The Basics: Adding Color, p. 29).

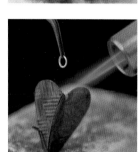

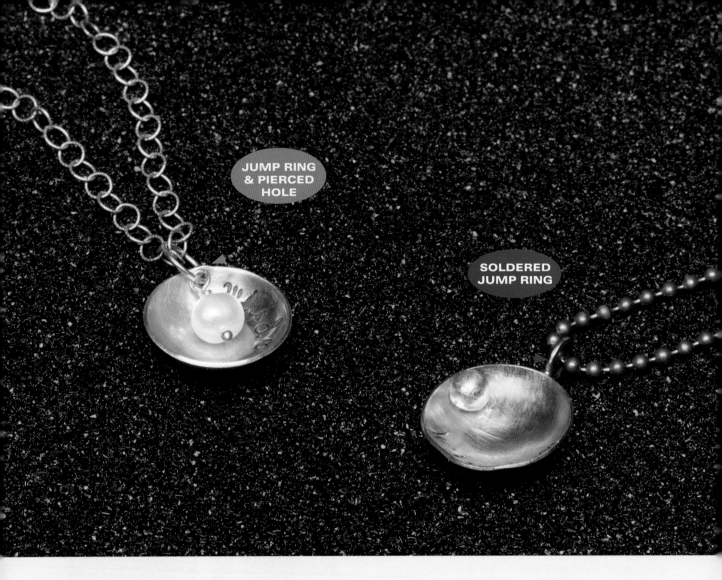

JUMP RING & PIERCED HOLE

SOLDERED JUMP RING

Pearl of Wisdom pendants

Both of these projects will satisfy the desire for instant gratification in all of us. Quick, easy, and low-tech, this pendant will give you practice in basic skills: stamping, wire wrapping, and dapping. The hot project is an easy soldering project that also includes balling up fine silver with a torch.

TOOLS & SUPPLIES

- metal alphabet stamps or decorative stamps
- rawhide or nylon mallet
- bench block
- screw-down punch
- roundnose pliers
- wire cutters
- chainnose pliers
- flatnose pliers

MATERIALS

- 24-gauge, .75" (19mm) silver disk
- 4mm pearl
- 18-gauge 6mm OD jump ring
- ball-end sterling silver headpin, 1.50" (38mm)
- necklace chain

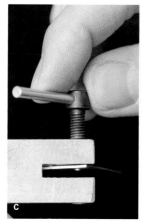

If you would like to add a little texture to the disk, strike the ball-peen face of a chasing hammer on the surface **[A]**. Hammer uniformly and lightly around the disk to avoid distorting the shape. Texturing before stamping a design or word will ensure that the letters are not distorted.

Stamp your words in a curve along the edge of the disk (refer to The Basics: Metal Stamping, p. 27) **[B]**. If one of your letters has a descender (such as the tail on a lowercase "y"), keep the other letters away from the edge to allow enough space for the descender.

Punch a hole at the top of the disk, centered relative to your text **[C]**. Punching the hole after stamping gives you margin for error—you can avoid the letters running into the hole.

Dap the disk in a wood dapping set with the text facing up to minimize the possibility of damaging the stampings **[D, E]**. Add patina and polish as desired (refer to The Basics: Adding Color, p. 29).

Wire-wrap a pearl onto a sterling silver headpin and attach it to the metal dome with a jump ring. (refer to The Basics: Wrapped Loops with Beads, p. 20). Hang on a necklace chain.

TOOLS & SUPPLIES

- wire cutters
- metal alphabet stamps or decorative stamps
- rawhide or nylon mallet
- bench block
- third hand
- steel wool
- soldering setup
- copper paste solder

MATERIALS

- 24-gauge, .75" (19mm) copper, silver, or brass disk
- 18-gauge fine-silver wire or scrap fine silver, 1" (25.5mm)
- 20-gauge 6mm OD copper, silver, or brass jump ring
- necklace chain

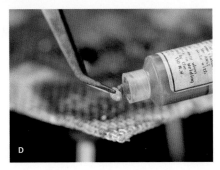

Stamp your text or design onto a disk. Dome the disk. Create a "pearl" from fine silver: Place the fine-silver wire or scrap on a charcoal or magnesia block. Heat the metal directly with the torch until a granule (ball) forms **[A, B]**. If you want a larger ball, add more silver pieces, place them near the ball, and heat again. Quench in cool water.

Remove any charcoal or magnesia residue from the ball with steel wool **[C]**. Place a 2mm dab of copper paste solder on the back of the silver pearl, and place it anywhere on the disk away from the stampings **[D]**.

➜ **TIP** A charcoal block is the traditional surface for creating granules, but magnesia is cheaper and less messy.

Heat the entire unit and then the granule until the solder flows **[E, F]**. If the granule doesn't adhere to the disk but the solder has flowed onto the disk, the granule may not have been hot enough to allow the solder to flow evenly. Remember, solder follows heat; if the disk is hotter than the granule, it will not solder properly. If necessary, apply a little flux to help the solder flow. Reheat, this time getting enough heat onto the granule. If the granule slips, hold the disk at an angle with firesafe tweezers opposite the granule until the solder flows **[G]**.

Clamp the disk vertically in a third hand or crosslocking tweezers, and place over a tripod with mesh. Apply a 2mm dab of copper solder to the top of the disk. Use firesafe tweezers to hold the jump ring above the solder **[H]**. With the torch, begin heating the disk (but not the jump ring) **[I]**. The residual heat will be enough for the solder to flow. (If you overheat the jump ring, the solder will flow up into the ring and will not make the connection.)

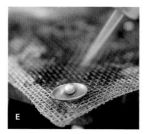

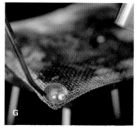

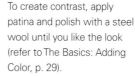

Direct the heat to a point on the disk below where the jump ring will solder **[J]**. When the solder flows between the jump ring and disk, remove the heat and take a deep breath (allowing a moment for the solder to set) **[K]**. Remove the tweezers.

Quench in cool water, and pickle. Remove the piece from the pickle after the oxidation has dissolved, and rinse it in clean water.

To create contrast, apply patina and polish with a steel wool until you like the look (refer to The Basics: Adding Color, p. 29).

SOLDERED
LAYERS

TUBE
RIVETS

Flourish bracelets

In this project, you don't need to limit yourself to flowers—you can use any metal shapes you find pleasing. Watch gears or metal scraps are great in this bracelet. You can adapt the project to make earrings or pendants too. Add chain links between the main shapes instead of jump rings for an entirely different look.

In the cold-connection project, you will learn how to make connections with tube rivets. With so many pieces to complete, you will have plenty of opportunity to practice this technique. The hot project is simply fun; watching pieces of silver turn into balls is entertaining! You will make at least 18 silver granules that will become hot connection points on the flowers.

TOOLS & SUPPLIES
- burnisher (optional)
- rawhide or nylon-head mallet
- bench block
- metal design stamps (optional)
- screw-down punch
- steel dapping set
- center punch
- finishing punch
- Sharpie

MATERIALS
7" (17.8CM) BRACELET
- 24-gauge, 0.75" (19mm)-diameter brass disks, 7–8
- copper flowers in various sizes, 10–14
- vintage metal pieces, 6–8
- 2x3mm copper tubes, 13
- 6mm 20-gauge copper jump rings, 7–8
- 6mm 18-gauge copper jump rings, 2
- Copper S-hook

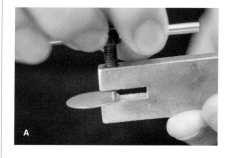
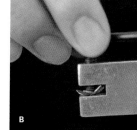
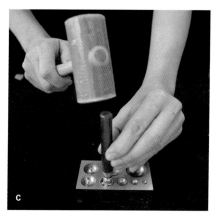

Following the template, pierce a hole on opposite sides of each brass disk using the smaller screw of the screw-down punch. (A 1.25mm round hand punch may also be used.) Punch the holes close to the edges so you can insert the jump rings and the disks will have room to move **[A]**.

→ **TIP** To lengthen the bracelet, add another brass disk. If adding a disk makes the bracelet too long, add extra jump rings between the disks.

Using the large (black) screw of the punch, pierce a large hole in the center of each flower and vintage piece **[B].** Dap each copper flower using a steel dapping block, a punch, and a rawhide or nylon-head mallet. Place the flower into a divot that is slightly smaller than the flower; choose a dapping punch that fits into the dap, and strike the punch with the mallet, forcing the flower to cup **[C, D]**.

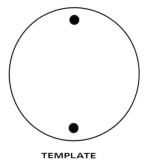

TEMPLATE

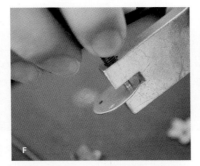

Place the decorative metal pieces on the brass disk to mark holes for connections **[E]**. Pierce a large hole (black screw) at each mark on each brass disk **[F]**.

Stamp the brass disks to add texture as desired before connecting any metal pieces (refer to The Basics: Metal Stamping, p. 27). Add patina if desired (refer to The Basics: Adding Color, p. 29).

Connect the flower pieces first: Place a 2x3mm piece of tubing on end on a bench block. With a center punch directly on the tube, gently tap the center punch with a riveting hammer until the end is flared. Flip the tube over on the flared end **[G, right]** and place a brass disk over it **[H]**. Add a flower **[I]**. The flower on the left shows a nearly finished tube rivet.

Flare the other end of the tube in the same way **[J]**. With a finishing punch, flatten the tube rivet until the pieces are secure **[K]**. The rivet on the left has been flattened; the rivet on the right has been flared but not flattened. If you do not have a finishing punch, you can use a small dapping punch from a metal dapping set. Repeat until all sets of pieces are riveted in this way. Connect the disks with jump rings. Add a jump ring on one end as the loop and attach the S-hook to the other end.

TOOLS & SUPPLIES

- burnisher (optional)
- rawhide or nylon-head mallet
- bench block
- metal design stamps (optional)
- steel dapping set
- screw-down punch
- soldering setup with magnesia block
- copper paste solder

MATERIALS

- 24-gauge, 0.75" (19mm)-diameter brass disks, 7–8
- copper flowers in various sizes, 16
- 24-gauge fine-silver wire, 16" (40.6cm)
- copper S-hook or 2" (51mm) 16-gauge copper wire to make your own

Pierce holes in the brass disks and dap all of the flowers as in the cold-connection project. (Refer to the hot Pearl of Wisdom pendant project, p. 52, for additional information on making and soldering granules.) Make silver granules for each of the flowers you will be using from fine silver: Cut 1" (25.5mm) pieces of 24-gauge wire, place the wire on a charcoal or magnesia block, and heat the pieces directly until a granule or ball forms. If you want a larger ball, add more silver pieces and heat again. Quench in cool water. Remove any residue from the balls with steel wool.

Place a brass disk on the mesh on the tripod. Place copper paste solder on the bottom of each flower at the hole **[A]**. (You will be able to solder both granule and the flower to the disk at the same time.) Place a silver granule in the middle of each flower **[B]**. Heat the entire unit until all pieces are evenly hot, moving the torch around the unit continuously until the solder flows **[C, D]**. Allow the solder a moment to set **[E]**.

Quench in cool water, and pickle. Repeat to solder all of the flowers onto the disks, and then quench, pickle, rinse, and dry each piece. If the pieces aren't as clean as you'd like, use a brass-bristle brush and water to clean the surfaces. For a higher polish, use a brass brush in a flex shaft.

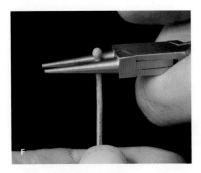

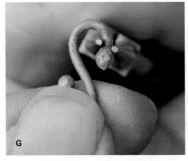

Draw a 3mm ball on each end of the 16-gauge copper wire by holding the wire vertically with a pair of firesafe tweezers in your dominant hand. Using the torch with your nondominant hand, point the flame at the end of the wire, making sure that the wire is at or just past the tip of the inner blue cone. If you are too close or too far from the flame, the wire will not ball efficiently. As soon as you are in the sweet spot, you will immediately see the ball start to form.

As the ball forms, follow it up the wire with the flame. Quench, rinse, and dry the wire.

To create an S-clasp: With roundnose pliers, make a loop at each end of the wire, turning them in opposite directions to create an S shape with each end touching the centerpoint **[F, G]**. Hammer the large curves of the S. This will harden the metal to keep the clasp from coming apart **[H]**.

Connect the flower units using copper jump rings and two pairs of pliers. Add the hook on one end and a jump ring on the other end.

balling wire ends
Making balled-end headpins efficiently is all about how you position the torch relative to the wire.

Just right

Too close

Too far

TUBE
RIVET

SOLDERED
BANDS

Spinning rings

Of this pair, the hot project is easier and faster to accomplish, so you may consider trying that version first. The cold project will give you experience with making sheet metal flare as you shape it with a hammer. I suggest you start with copper, pay attention to every movement, and make corrections to your technique along the way.

TOOLS & SUPPLIES

- bezel shears, straight
- burnisher
- files
- rawhide or nylon-head mallet
- horn anvil
- dividers
- screw-down punch
- Sharpie
- steel ring mandrel (stepped mandrel preferred)
- forming block or thick telephone book
- nylon-jaw pliers
- chasing hammer
- riveting hammer
- center punch

MATERIALS

- 24-gauge textured brass sheet metal, 5x3" (12.7cmx76mm)
- 24-gauge textured copper sheet metal, 1x3" (25.5x76mm)
- copper tubing, 2x3mm

Determine the minimum length of sheet metal needed by using the chart on p. 61 and add .25" (6.5mm). Open the dividers to 1" (25.5mm) or the desired width for the ring, and score the back of the textured copper sheet **[A]**. Cut with bezel shears **[B]**.

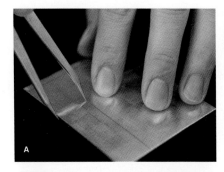

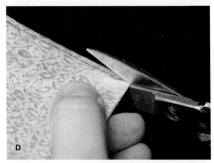

This piece will be longer than the final project, which will allow some room for adjustment. Wider rings must be a little bigger than the usual size.

Close the dividers to approximately .13" (3mm), score a piece of brass **[C]**, and cut with shears **[D]**.

Burnish and flatten the edges of both pieces (refer to The Basics: Cutting and Piercing Metal, p. 23). Straighten the brass strip with a pair of nylon-jaw pliers (the edges may be sharp; wear a glove and use caution) **[E]**.

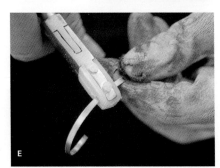

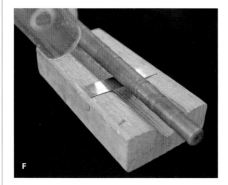

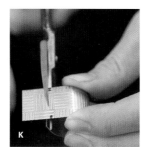

how much metal?
If a ring size is 0, your metal will need to be 1.44" (37mm) long. For every quarter size up from 0, add .6mm until you reach the size you need; add the thickness of the metal.

If math is not your strong suit, do what I do and cut more than enough and trim after forming around the mandrel.

Here are some standard measurements showing inside circumference of rings and the corresponding U.S. size.

Inside circumference	Size
1.94" (49mm)	5
2" (51mm)	5½
2.04" (51.2mm)	6
2.10" (53mm)	6½
2.14" (54mm)	7
2.20" (56mm)	7½
2.24" (57mm)	8
2.30" (59mm)	8½
2.34" (59.5mm)	9
2.40" (61mm)	9½
2.44" (62mm)	10

Place the copper strip (the shank) on a forming block **[F]**. (Don't have a forming block? See the following page.) Place a stepped ring mandrel over the metal at the correct size.

→ **TIP** A tapered steel ring mandrel will also work, although it is more difficult to use. If you are using a standard mandrel, you will need to flip the ring shank back and forth while forming the ring to avoid forming a cone.

With a rawhide or nylon-head mallet, strike directly onto the ring mandrel—hard. This will force the metal to form around the mandrel **[G]**. Working from the sides, tap down the metal to form the ring around the mandrel **[H]**. Flip the shank over if you cannot work from both sides. For those who have strong hands and fingers, you may opt to force the metal down with your fingers **[I]**.

With the ends overlapping, mark the metal, leaving a .19" (5mm) gap **[J]**. Trim with bezel shears **[K]**.

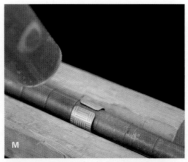

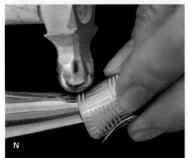

Create your own forming block

Forming blocks of varying sizes may be purchased, but they are easily made if you have access to a circular saw. I know this sounds crazy, but check with your neighbors! Aside from my power drill, my cordless circular saw is my absolute favorite power tool. I think every girl should own one.

You will need a scrap piece of 2x4" (51mmx10.2cm) wood about 12" (30.5cm) long. Don't have one lying around your studio? Go to the nearest hardware/lumber store and they surely will have a bucket full of scrap (usually free). Pick up a few pieces; scrap wood is handy to have around your workbench. You may not have a use for it now, but you will.

Cut two 45-degree angles into the middle of the wood block and *voila*! You have a forming block.

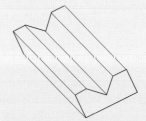

Here's another option: Pull a telephone book out of the recycle bin. The thicker the book, the better. Open it to the middle and you have an instant forming block! Not the best, but it works.

Snip the corners **[L]**, and file and sand them until they are rounded. If the shape is a little distorted from the trimming and filing, place the ring back onto the mandrel and reform it **[M]**.

Holding the ring shank at a 30-degree angle on a horn anvil, tap the shank just above the bottom edge with the ball-peen end of a chasing hammer **[N]**. This will force the metal to bend outward, curving the middle **[O]**. Be patient; this process will require you to gradually shape, move, and repeat many times. Continue working around the shank as many times as you need to achieve the flare desired. Then repeat on the other edge. To keep distortion minimal, strike the metal evenly throughout the process.

→ **TIP** When tapping the metal, make deliberate moves. Too many taps will work-harden the ring, making it difficult to work. You can anneal the metal to soften it for forming, but keep in mind you'll need to pickle and repolish the metal (refer to The Basics: Annealing and Soldering, p 30).

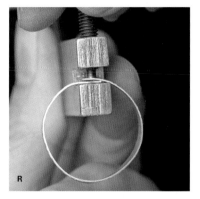

If the edges have distorted from hammering, file again as needed to remove any sharpness. Sand the ends further if they are still sharp. Wrap the strip of brass around the shank to measure for size **[P]**. Overlap the ends at least .16" (4mm) to hold a rivet. Mark the point of overlap **[Q]** and snip with shears. File and smooth the cut ends of the brass.

With the ends overlapping as before, make a large hole with a screw-down punch through both ends **[R]**. If your punch cannot cut through two pieces of metal, punch one piece, tape the pieces together, and, using the first hole as a guide, punch the second piece to ensure that the holes match up properly. Wrap the brass band around the shank.

Stand a 2x3mm copper tube on end on an anvil or bench block. With a center punch directly on the tube, gently tap the center punch in a circular motion until the tube is flared on one side (refer to The Basics: Tube Rivets, p. 25) **[S]**. Flip the tube over and place it through the holes in the brass band from underneath **[T]**.

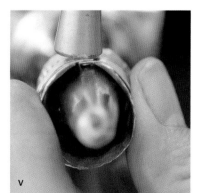

Carefully place the entire unit on the flat side of the horned anvil **[U]**. With a riveting hammer and center punch, tap on the tube to flare it. When both sides are evenly flared, finish the rivet by tapping directly onto the rivet with the face of the riveting hammer **[V]**.

TOOLS & SUPPLIES

- bezel shears, straight
- burnisher
- files
- rawhide or nylon-head mallet
- dividers
- Sharpie
- steel ring mandrel
- steel dap and block set
- forming block or thick telephone book
- flatnose pliers
- sandpaper, 500-grit
- steel wool
- soldering setup
- copper paste solder

MATERIALS

- 20-gauge brass sheet, 1x3" (25.5x76cm)
- 24-gauge textured copper sheet, 0.25x3" (6.5x76cm)

Refer to the cold connection project to prepare the metal strips. First, determine the length of the brass strip using the information on p. 61. Open the dividers to .75" (19mm) or the desired width, score the brass, and cut it with bezel shears. If you are not strong enough to cut the metal, use a jeweler's saw. Close the dividers to approximately .13" (3mm), and score a sheet of copper texture sheet on the back. Cut the strip and straighten it with nylon-jaw pliers.

Place the brass strip on a forming block. Form the strip around the ring mandrel. Flip the ring back and forth if you cannot work from both sides **[A, B]**.

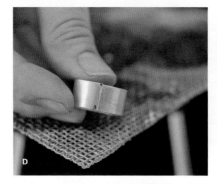
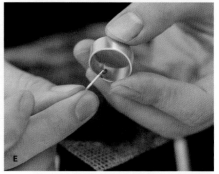

Use a rawhide or nylon-head mallet to hammer the strip until the ends meet. Mark and cut the excess metal with bezel shears. Place the ring shank back into the mandrel and continue hammering until the edges meet perfectly **[C]**. If your cut was not perfect, file the ends to make them align perfectly. If they do not, there will be gaps in the soldered seam. Tighten the ends together, overlapping them slightly, to allow the tension in the metal to hold the ends tightly together, and pull the metal back into place **[D]**.

Place a couple of dabs of copper paste solder on the inside of the ring shank **[E]**. Place the shank seam-side down on the soldering surface. If the ring shank rolls on the soldering surface, shape the shank into an oval or use steel pins to help it stay in place while soldering.

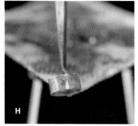

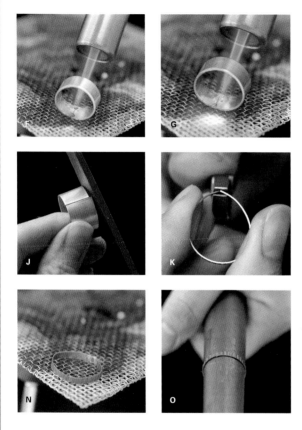

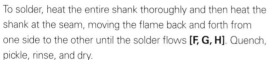

Using the brass ring shank to measure, bend the textured copper strip loosely around the shank. Cut the strip to size with bezel shears.

Anneal the copper strip to keep it from springing back. To anneal, heat the metal with the torch until it has a rosy glow, then quench in cool water immediately. This should soften the metal enough to make it easier to bend into place. To help bring the ends together, hold the join together with one hand and pinch the ends flat with a pair of flatnose pliers **[K, L]**. The ends must meet and stay in place by tension (without help) to be able to solder **[M]**.

Place copper paste solder on the inside of the ring. Solder to create a narrow ring **[N]**. Quench in cool water. Pickle both pieces until clean. Rinse in clean water and dry with a rag.

Reshape the copper ring as necessary on the ring mandrel **[O]**.

To solder, heat the entire shank thoroughly and then heat the shank at the seam, moving the flame back and forth from one side to the other until the solder flows **[F, G, H]**. Quench, pickle, rinse, and dry.

You can easily reshape the ring shank if necessary by placing it back on the ring mandrel and tapping directly onto it with a rawhide or nylon-head mallet until it is round again. Looking down the mandrel, you should be able to identify the warped areas of the shank **[I]**. If the ends are uneven, file until you remove any jagged edges **[J]**.

Sand the inside and outside of the brass shank to remove any excess solder. Wrap a piece of sandpaper around a wood mandrel or dowel to assist sanding the inside of the shank **[P]**. If there are sharp edges around the shank, use sandpaper to smooth them. To finish polishing the brass and copper shanks, use steel wool, a brass-bristle brush, or a brass brush on a flex shaft **[Q]**. (For more polishing options refer to The Basics: Polishing, p. 36.)

Place the brass ring shank into the copper ring on top of a bench block. Place a steel dapping punch that is slightly wider than the ring shank on top of the shank. With a rawhide or nylon-head mallet, dap the brass ring until it begins to flare **[R]**. Flip the unit over, and dap again. Continue this action until the copper ring cannot slip off of the brass ring. Be sure to dap both sides evenly **[S]**.

TUBE
RIVETS

SOLDERED
FRAME

Pod pendants

Both cold and hot pods can be created in any size that suits your taste. Both projects are very forgiving. Make the cold project big or small to hold pearls or beads you like. In the hot project, you can easily create different sizes of granules by adding silver and heating it.

Choose the cold project for tube-riveting practice and the chance to add color with beads. The hot project will hone your step-soldering skills.

TOOLS & SUPPLIES

- bezel shears, straight
- burnisher
- files
- rawhide or nylon-head mallet
- bench knife or butter knife
- chainnose pliers
- flatnose pliers
- bench block
- screw-down punch
- goldsmith's hammer
- Sharpie
- paper
- acetone
- cotton pad or swab
- liver of sulfur (optional)
- steel wool or polishing pads

MATERIALS

- 24-gauge copper sheet, 1x6" (25.5mmx15.2cm)
- 24-gauge copper wire, 16" (40.6cm)
- 2x3mm copper tubes, 2
- pearls or beads in various sizes, 3
- 24-gauge wire (scrap), 4" (10.2cm)

There are many approaches to creating a pod. You can draw one with paper and pencil, create one with a drawing program on your computer, or wing it ... like I do. Make your pattern slightly smaller than your goal; you'll create texture after you cut the metal, which will make it "grow."

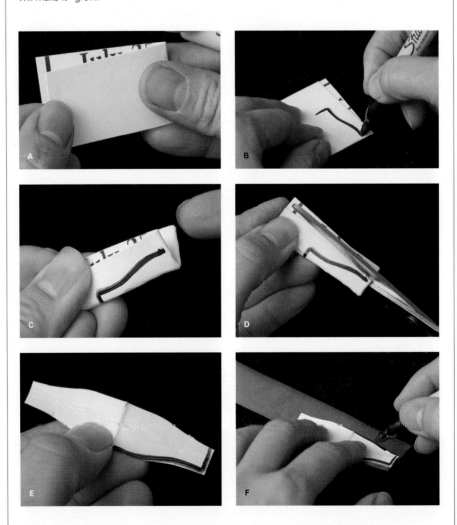

Fold a small piece of paper in half and draw one side of the pod shape. Fold in half again lengthwise, and, using the first cut as a guide, cut through all the layers **[A–D]**. Open to see the pattern **[E]**. Trim as necessary. Trace the pattern onto sheet metal with a Sharpie **[F]**.

Cut using bezel shears. Trim as desired (refer to The Basics: Cutting and Piercing Metal, p. 23).

Using the metal piece that you just cut as a pattern, trace and cut a second piece from the metal **[G]**. This will ensure that the pieces match. Remove any leftover ink with acetone and cotton **[H]**. Flatten both pieces with a rawhide or nylon-head mallet on the bench block.

To create texture, use the cross-peen face of a goldsmith's hammer, striking as shown to create hash marks on one side of each piece **[I]**. The displacement of metal from hammering will cause the metal to curl. Use a rawhide or nylon-head mallet to flatten both pieces again **[J]**.

Mark the wrong side of both pieces **[K]** and tape them together around the center of the shape with the marks facing each other **[L]**. If the edges do not meet, file and trim until they are even.

Mark and punch a hole at each end of the pod shape using the large side of the screw-down punch. Punch the hole .25" (6.5mm) from the edge **[M]**. If your punch cannot cut

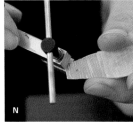

through two pieces of metal, punch one piece, tape the pieces together, and use the first hole as a guide to punch the second piece. This will ensure that the holes match up properly **[N]**.

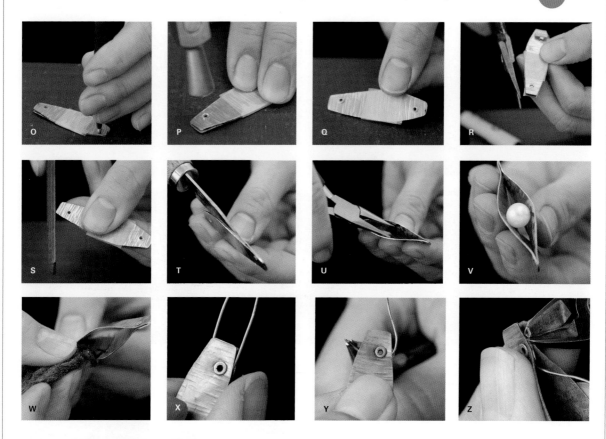

Rivet the two metal pieces together with 3mm tubes (refer to The Basics: Tube Rivets, p. 25) **[O, P, Q]**. Trim the pieces with bezel shears so they match **[R]**. File as needed to make the sides even and create a shape you like **[S]**. With a bench knife or a butter knife, carefully separate the metal pieces **[T]**. If you did a good job riveting, the ends will stay connected. Be careful not to force the metal too much; this may cause scratches.

Use flatnose pliers to separate the pieces enough to accommodate your pearls or beads. Make the back opening narrower than the front **[U, V]**. Remove any markings with acetone or steel wool **[W]**. Polish with steel wool until you achieve the desired effect.

Use liver of sulfur solution to add patina to the pod. Cut a 4" (10.2cm) piece of 24-gauge wire, make a hook on the end, and use it to help you dip the piece into the solution (refer to The Basics: Adding Color, p. 29). Remove the wire and clean the inside and outside of the piece with steel wool.

Cut a 16" (40.6cm) piece of 24-gauge wire and remove any kinks by drawing it through a pair of nylon-jaw pliers. Feed 2" (51mm) of wire between the metal pieces at one end and create an uneven U shape, pulling tightly toward the rivet **[X]**. Working in a circular motion, wind the short end of the wire around the rivet. Use chainnose pliers to hold the wire; this will help you pull tightly **[Y]**. Wind at least twice around the rivet. Trim the short wire and tuck it inside the pod **[Z]**.

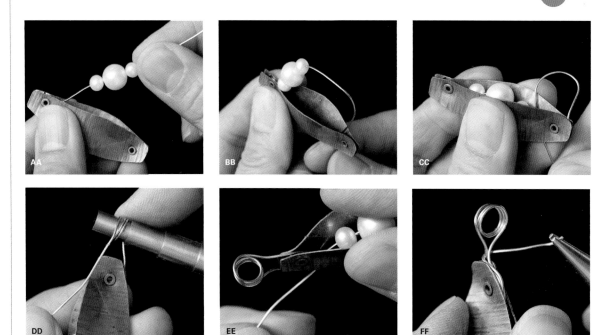

Slide pearls or beads onto the long end of the wire. Slide them inside the pod **[AA]**. Wrap the long wire once around the opposite rivet **[BB, CC]**.

Create a loop with the excess wire by wrapping it three times around a mini stepped mandrel about .31" (8mm) above the pod **[DD]**. Insert the end of the wire into the pod, pulling up tightly as the wire exits the pod, but without shortening the bail **[EE]**. Bring the wire around the base of the bail and continue wrapping the wire around the stem of the bail, working your way toward the loops **[FF]**. Use your fingers or pliers. Stop wrapping when you reach the base of the loops. Trim any excess wire and tuck in the remaining tail with pliers.

For an interesting bail, separate the wires by inserting a knife between them and twisting slightly to spread the loops **[GG]**.

TOOLS & SUPPLIES

- bezel shears, curved
- burnisher
- files
- heavy-duty wire cutters or jeweler's saw
- rawhide or nylon-head mallet
- bench block
- paper
- Sharpie
- soldering setup
- hard, medium, and easy silver paste solder
- liver of sulfur (optional)
- steel wool or polishing pads

MATERIALS

- 24-gauge sterling silver sheet, 1.5x.75" (38x19cm)
- 10-gauge sterling silver square wire, 4" (10.2cm) (approx.)
- fine-silver wire or scrap (amount varies)
- sterling silver tube, 4mm, .25" (6.5mm)

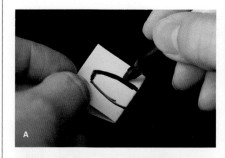

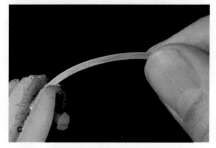

Create a pattern for your pod by drawing half the shape on a folded piece of paper **[A]**. Try not to worry about making the perfect pattern; an irregular shape is great for this design. Trace the pattern onto 24-gauge sterling silver sheet with a Sharpie **[B]**.

→ TIP The pod shape can be any size you like. If you make a large pod, you will need to create large peas to fit inside, which requires more silver. You may want to make the peas first and then cut the pod to fit your peas.

Using curved bezel shears, trim the sheet metal to shape. If necessary, flatten the metal with a rawhide or nylon-head mallet on a bench block.

With a pair of nylon-jaw pliers and your fingers, bend a piece of 10-gauge sterling silver square wire to match the curve of one side of the pod **[C]**.

Trim the wire with a pair of heavy-duty flush cutters (or use a jeweler's saw) to match the edge of the metal shape **[D]**.

Cut a second piece of square wire, bend the wire the same way, and trim the end so it butts up against the other wire when placed on the pod base **[E]**. The wires must also lie flat on the cut sheet metal; if necessary, flatten them down with a rawhide or nylon-head mallet on a steel bench block.

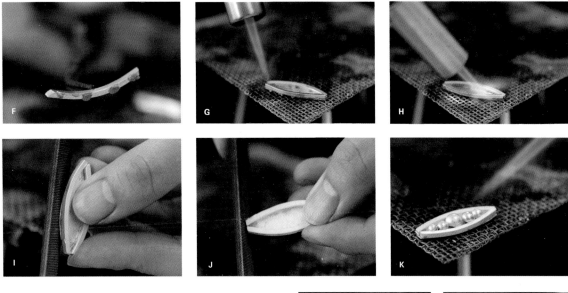

Put the unit on a tripod with a steel screen. Place dabs of hard solder under each square wire **[F]**. Place the wires on the pod base and solder both wires to the base in one operation. Keep the flame moving around the unit from the top to enable the solder to flow evenly **[G]**. When the solder begins to flow, aim the flame at the sides to bring the solder through the join **[H]**.

Quench in cool water, and pickle until the firescale has dissolved. Rinse in clean water and dry.

File the base so it's flush with the square wire. **[I]**. (Be careful not to file into the wire.) File one end of the pod so you can attach the tube as a bail **[J]**. If the tube is too wide, saw or file it to size.

Make 5–7 granules of varying sizes from fine silver (refer to the Pearl of Wisdom pendants project, p. 50, for instruction). If the granule is not large enough, place more silver next to the original ball, and heat again.

→ **TIP** **If you want the granules to be flat on top, arrange them in the pod and gently strike them with a chasing hammer. This will expand the peas, so check the fit.**

Dab a little medium paste solder on the bottom of each granule. Arrange the granules in the pod. Heat the entire pod from all directions thoroughly until the solder flows and the granules are attached **[K]**. Quench, pickle, and rinse.

Grasp a tube with tweezers and put some easy solder along one side **[L]**. Place the tube at the top of the pod, making sure the pieces are touching. Solder by first heating the entire pod until it is evenly hot **[M]**, and then concentrate the heat at the top of the pod along the tube until the solder flows. Because the tube is a smaller piece, if you overheat it, the solder will tend to flow to the tube, and it will not adhere to the pod.

Quench. Pickle until the piece is white and clean. Polish as desired (refer to The Basics: Polishing, p. 36).

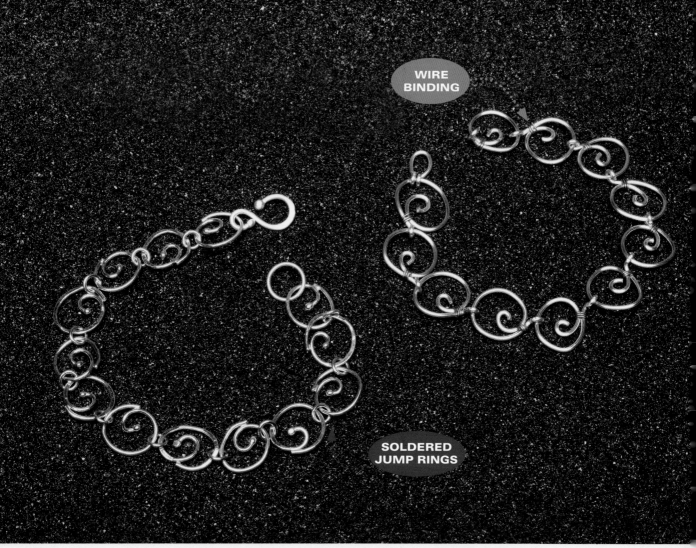

WIRE BINDING

SOLDERED JUMP RINGS

Spiral Chain bracelets

Binding with wire is a useful connection technique. Tight wire wraps can be an attractive accent in metal and beaded creations.

Both cold and hot bracelets will give you practice making wire spirals. Repeating the motion will create muscle memory, and soon you'll be making the perfect spiral every time. The cold project will give you a good understanding of binding and how pieces can stay together with wire. The hot project will help you learn how to solder in tight spots and give you practice making balled-end headpins. I bet you'll immediately be addicted to making these useful components!

TOOLS & SUPPLIES

- nylon-jaw pliers
- wire cutters
- files or cup bur
- roundnose pliers
- chainnose pliers
- flatnose pliers
- mini step mandrel
- ruler

MATERIALS
7.25" (18.4CM)
BRACELET

- 18-gauge wire, 1 yd. (91.4cm)
- 24-gauge wire in contrasting color, 1 yd.

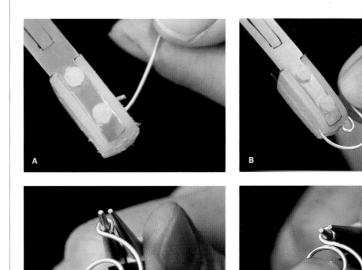

Straighten the 18-gauge wire and cut it into 2.50" (64mm) pieces. Use roundnose pliers to make a loop that will be the center of the spiral. Grasp the loop with nylon-jaw pliers and turn the wire in a circular motion to create a spiral **[A]**. Reposition the wire in the jaws as you continue to turn **[B]**.

→ **TIP** Making perfect spirals takes practice. If this is your first time, give yourself a break and make a few test spirals with inexpensive copper wire.

Continue spiraling until there is about .50" (13mm) of wire left. With roundnose pliers, grasp the other end of the wire at the very tip and make a loop in the opposite direction **[C]**. Push the small loop close to the spiral **[D]**. Make enough spirals for your desired bracelet length, taking into account the length of the clasp; I made 11.

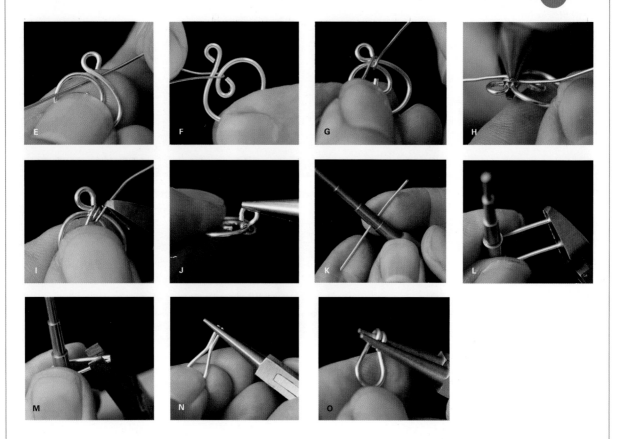

→ **TIP** I used copper wire as the binding wire to create contrast with the 18-gauge silver wire.

Cut a 3" (76mm) piece of 24-gauge wire. Place the binding wire under the spiral at the join and bend the wire in half to make a U around the wire as shown **[E, F]**. Bring the wire around the base, pulling firmly in opposite directions to bind the spirals together **[G]**.

As you move the binding wire around the spiral, compress the wires with a pair of chainnose pliers to help snug the wires **[H]**. Go around three or four times. Trim any excess wire with wire cutters as closely as you can **[I]**. To prevent snagging when you wear the bracelet, squeeze down on the wire ends with chainnose pliers.

With chainnose pliers, turn the small loop up 90 degrees. This will act as your connection between links **[J]**.

Continue binding and bending the 90-degree connector loops for all of the links. Open the connector loops, attach the links consecutively, and close each loop in turn except for the last loop. This will become the loop of the clasp.

To create the hook part of the clasp, cut a 1.50" (38mm) piece of 18-gauge wire and use your fingers to form it into a U around a mini step mandrel or roundnose pliers **[K]**. Trim with wire cutters to make both ends even **[L]**. Pinch the ends together with flatnose pliers **[M]**. Remove the wire from the mandrel and form the open ends around roundnose pliers **[N, O]**. Attach this part to the last link.

TOOLS & SUPPLIES

- wire cutters
- files or cup bur
- roundnose pliers
- chainnose pliers
- flatnose pliers
- tumbler with stainless steel shot
- easy paste solder
- soldering setup

MATERIALS
8" (20.3CM) BRACELET

- 18-gauge fine-silver wire, 24" (61cm)
- 16-gauge fine-silver wire, 1.75" (44mm)
- 19-gauge 8mm OD sterling silver jump ring
- 19-gauge 6mm sterling silver jump rings, 12

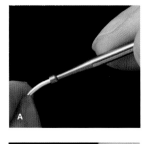

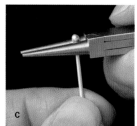
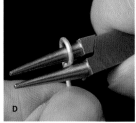
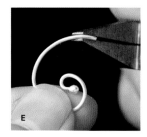

Cut all of the 18-gauge fine-silver wire into 2" (51mm) pieces using wire cutters (use flush cutters if you have them). Ball up one end of each wire and quench each piece of wire entirely as you progress (refer to p. 58 for detailed instructions).

CAUTION! Heat spreads through metal. Quench the entire wire before handling.

You can create a ball of almost any size, but keep in mind that a ball that is too big and heavy will fall off as gravity takes over. The larger the ball you create, the shorter the wire will become, resulting in a smaller link and a smaller bracelet. Start with an extra .25" (6.5mm) of wire if you want a larger ball.

If you find that you are creating little pins at the end of your balls, this is because you have pulled the wire away from the flame too soon. To correct, just reheat until the pin disappears.

If the non-balled ends of the wire are sharp, use a cup bur **[A]** or a needle file to smooth them **[B]**.

Grasp the wire at the base of the ball with roundnose pliers. Roll the pliers to create a tight loop **[C, D]**. As in the cold project, grasp the loop with nylon-jaw pliers and form a loose spiral: Turn and bend the wire, release your grasp, reposition the spiral in the pliers, and continue spiraling. Grasp the wire end with flatnose pliers **[E]** and bend it to touch the side of the spiral as shown **[F]**. This will be your soldering connection point, so the pieces must meet perfectly. Make enough spirals for your desired length; I made 13.

→ TIP If you have a hard time making spirals, consider an amoeba shape or a wonky square. Whatever you decide on, form consistent links and your bracelet will look great.

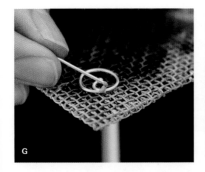
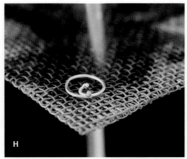
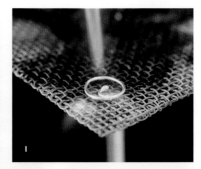

Place a spiral on a fire brick or a tripod with steel screen. Place a 2mm dab of hard solder at the point where the outside wire meets the spiral **[G]**. (To help you see the solder, the photo show more than the necessary amount.) Heat the spiral in a constant circular motion until the entire spiral has been evenly heated **[H]**. Continue in a circular motion, slowing when you reach the join at every pass until the solder flows **[I]**.

→ **TIP** It will take longer to read the last two paragraphs than it will take to solder a spiral!

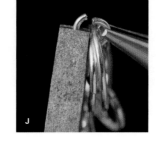
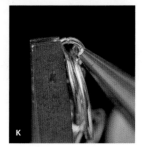

Do not take the metal past the orange-red color shown. Quench the spiral and continue soldering until you have soldered all of the spirals. Pickle and rinse all the pieces.

→ **TIP** When you are comfortable soldering and are able to identify the flow point, try placing your solder under the spiral instead of on the top. You will force the solder to flow up, which makes a cleaner join.

Using two pairs of chainnose or flatnose pliers (or one of each), open the jump rings and connect two spirals, making sure that the jump rings are closed tightly. Continue linking all of the spirals until you have the desired bracelet length, leaving a little room for the clasp. Place the 8mm jump ring on the last spiral for the loop part of the clasp **[J, K]**.

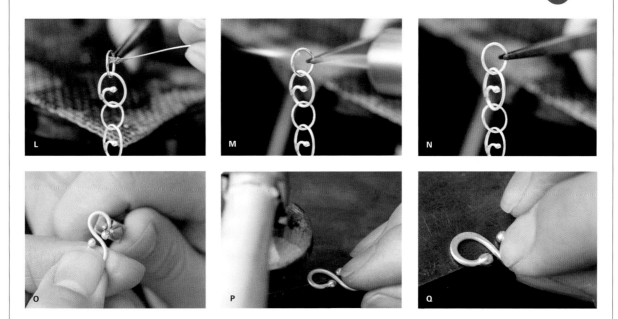

To solder the jump rings between the spirals, hold the jump ring with a pair of firesafe tweezers in your dominant hand with the opening either up or to the side, away from the tweezers. Warm the jump ring briefly with your torch flame to help the solder stick. Apply a 1mm dab of solder on the inside of the jump ring, under the opening **[L]**. Direct the flame slightly above the jump ring at the opening. This will draw the solder through the opening and seal it **[M]**. Watch for the solder to flow through the join **[N]**. Quench. As you work down through the links, quench between each soldering session to prevent burning yourself. Pickle and rinse.

Make a 3mm ball on each end of the 16-gauge wire. With roundnose pliers, make a loop at each end, turning them in opposite directions to create an S shape. Bend the ends so they touch the centerpoint of the S **[O]**.

Use a chasing hammer to hammer the large curves of the S-hook to harden the wire **[P, Q]**. This will keep the clasp from coming apart. Attach the S-hook to a spiral at one end of the bracelet.

➜ **TIP** You can add length by attaching additional jump rings between the clasp and the spiral.

WIRE
RIVETS

SOLDERED
RINGS

Wishes rings

Whether you make three, two, or just one ring, both cold and hot projects will teach
you to make simple rings that can be embellished easily. The cold project, teaches
how to use wire rivets as the connection, but for another look, try it with tube rivets.
The hot version will require attention to detail so the rings look seamless.

TOOLS & SUPPLIES

- flush wire cutters
- files
- ring mandrel
- screw-down punch
- chasing hammer or goldsmith's hammer
- riveting hammer
- horn anvil
- bench blocks, 2
- rawhide or nylon-head mallet

MATERIALS

- 12-gauge copper wire, 12" (30.5cm)
- 14-gauge sterling silver, 1" (25.5mm)

Determine your finished ring size and add a quarter size to accommodate the three interlocking rings. (If you make only one ring, you don't need to increase the size.) Using the information on. p. 61, calculate the length of wire you will need and add .25" (6.5mm). The extra length will allow for the overlap needed to rivet. If you don't like measuring, wrap the wire around the ring mandrel, adding enough for the overlap, and cut.

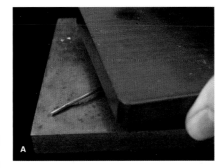

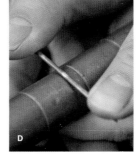

This wire will be too heavy to straighten with nylon-jaw pliers, so I suggest you use two bench blocks: Place the wire on a bench block, place the second block on top, apply pressure, and force the wire to roll under the bench block **[A]**. You can also carefully hammer your wire straight with a rawhide or nylon-head mallet.

Flatten both ends of the wire with a chasing hammer or goldsmith hammer. I prefer the goldsmith hammer because the head is a little smaller. Continue to hammer the ends until they are wider than the wire **[B]**. If a sharp edge has been created, file the sides to remove **[C]**.

Wrap the wire around a steel ring mandrel at the desired size **[D]**. If the wire is hard to work, use a rawhide or nylon-head mallet to shape it around the mandrel. Overlap the ends **[E]**. At this point you don't need to be too worried about making the shape perfect; you can do that after the ring has been riveted. Repeat to form two more rings.

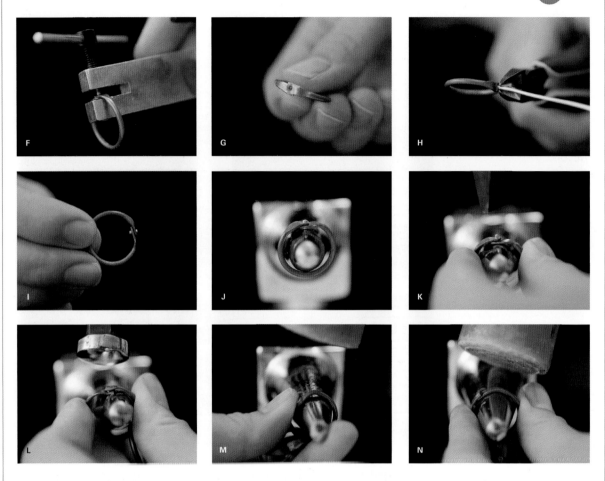

Pierce a hole through both ends of the overlapped wire with the large side of the screw-down punch **[F, G]**. Flush-cut the end of a piece of 14-gauge sterling silver wire, place it through both wires, and trim the end 1mm past where it exits **[H]**, leaving 1mm of wire extending from each side of the holes **[I]**. Gently place the assembly on an anvil horn **[J]**. (If you don't have an anvil, use a steel ring mandrel on a forming block.)

With the cross-peen face of your goldsmith's hammer, strike directly onto the wire end until it widens **[K]**. Finish by tapping directly on the wire with the flat face until the ring ends are locked into place **[L]**.

Interlock the second ring with the first ring, rivet in place, and repeat with the third.

If your rings have become distorted, place each ring individually onto the anvil or ring mandrel and carefully reshape while holding the other two rings away from the strike zone of the mallet **[M, N]**.

TOOLS & SUPPLIES

- flush wire cutters
- needle files
- ring mandrel
- horn anvil (optional)
- bench blocks, 2
- rawhide or nylon-head mallet
- soldering setup
- extra firesafe tweezers
- third hand
- hard, medium, and easy silver paste solder

MATERIALS

- 12-gauge half-round sterling silver wire, dead soft, 12" (30.5cm)

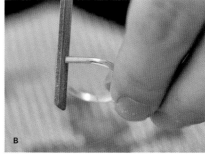

The 12-gauge half-round wire should be easy to manipulate, so begin forming a circle with your fingers. Wrap the wire around a stepped ring mandrel three times **[A]**. Cut all three wraps at once using flush cutters to help make all of the rings exactly the same size.

Carefully work the flush ends together until they are perfectly even. If your cutters have left a beveled end, use a needle file to make the ends meet flush **[B]**. The more perfectly your ends match, the less likely it is that you will see the seam. To force the ends together, squeeze them with a pair of flatnose pliers **[C, D]**. I promise, making a perfect circle will become easier as you practice **[E]**.

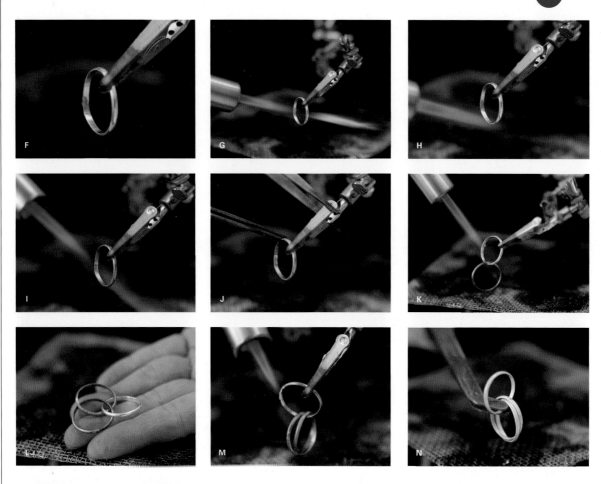

Place the ring in a third hand **[F]**. Place a 2mm dab of hard silver paste solder on the inside of the ring at the join. Move the torch around the entire ring, heating it evenly **[G]**, and then concentrate on either side of the seam **[H]**. If the seam is facing you, you will see the solder flow through it **[I]**.

Don't touch the third hand. To remove the ring from the third hand, use a pair or firesafe tweezers **[J]**. Interlock the second ring with the first. Place the join of the first ring as far as possible from the second join and solder it closed using medium paste solder **[K]**. Repeat to add the third ring using easy paste solder **[L, M]**.

Quench in cool water and pickle until all the rings are white **[N]**.

Sand each seam to remove any residual solder on the outside and inside of each ring, and then finish by polishing (refer to The Basics: Polishing, p. 36).

FILIGREE TABS

SOLDERED PRONGS

Harnessed pendants

You can set stones easily with tabs. In the cold project, you'll create tabs out of leaf and petal filigree shapes. If you already know how to rivet, this project should take less than half an hour. It makes a perfect quick gift.

The hot project will give you the freedom of designing from the back or the front. Working with wire, you can create a simple or intricate design to match the stone's character. Take advantage of clear cabochons by designing for both sides at the same time, or make the pendant reversible by positioning the bail in a strategic place.

TOOLS & SUPPLIES

- bezel shears, straight
- files
- riveting hammer
- bench block
- nylon-jaw pliers
- rawhide or nylon-head mallet
- Sharpie
- acetone
- cotton pad
- center punch

MATERIALS

- 25–45mm cabochon or flat bead of any shape
- 24-gauge copper sheet to fit the cab
- filigree flowers or leaves, 3–4
- 3mm copper tubes, 3–4
- 19-gauge 6mm OD copper jump rings, 3

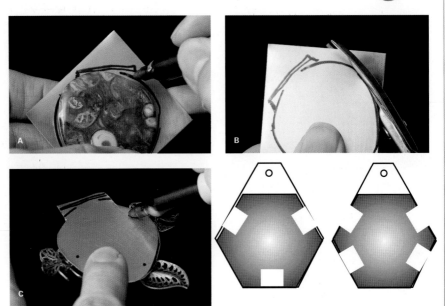

→ **TIP** The size, shape, and thickness of your cabochon will help you determine the size and number of filigree shapes you need to capture it. Make sure you'll have enough coverage around the cabochon and that there will not be a gap between the filigree shapes that will allow the cabochon to slip out. The shapes will need to be connected in the back with rivets and reach around the side of the stone to the front. The thicker your cabochon is, the larger the filigree shapes need to be.

Burnish the edges of the sheet metal. Place the cabochon on a piece of sheet metal close near the edges (to reduce work for later), leaving .25–.5" (6.5–13mm) near the top for the bail. Trace the cab with a Sharpie and draw a rough shape for the bail **[A]**.

Cut out the base with bezel shears. Trim it to size and file the edges to smooth any sharp edges **[B]**.

If your vintage pieces are not flat, flatten them on a bench block with a rawhide or nylon-head mallet. Place the vintage pieces on your work surface with the base on top to determine the placement of the rivets that will hold the tabs. Mark those points with a Sharpie **[C]**. Placement of the tabs is crucial to this project so the cabochon is secure. The illustration shows two ways of placing tabs for the same shape. As you plan, remember that the gap between tabs must be narrower than the stone.

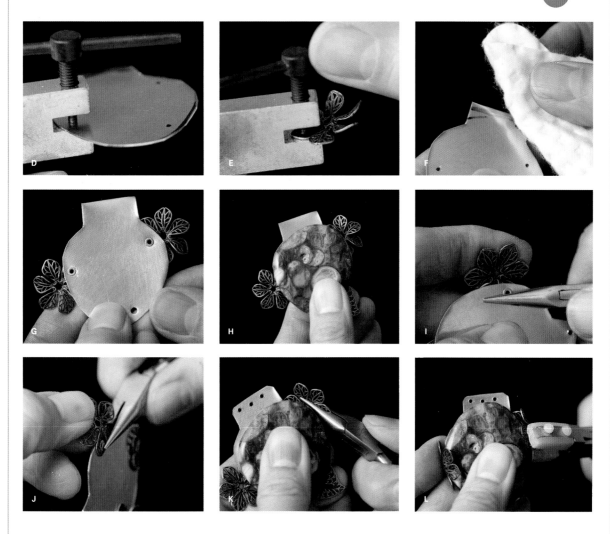

Pierce large (black) holes with a screw-down punch for the rivets in the metal base and in all of the filigree shapes **[D, E]**. Remove any remaining Sharpie marks with acetone and a cotton pad **[F]**.

Tube-rivet the vintage pieces right side down to the base to create the tabs **[G–H]** (refer to The Basics: Tube Rivets, p. 25). When you fold the tabs over the cabochon, the right side of the filigree will show. Pierce two or three small holes in the bail tab for jump rings.

Use chainnose pliers to tighten each tab against the base, folding the piece around the pliers to form a setting **[I, J]**. Place the cabochon on the base and continue to bend the tabs over the cabochon **[K]**. Gently secure all the tabs against the stone with nylon-jaw pliers **[L]**.

TOOLS & SUPPLIES

- flush wire cutters
- files
- roundnose pliers
- soldering setup
- hard, medium, and easy silver paste solder
- rotary tumbler (optional)

MATERIALS

- 18-gauge sterling silver wire, 12–18" (30.5–45.7cm)
- cabochon or stone

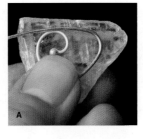
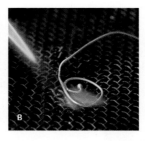

If you want balled ends on the wire for this pendant, ball the ends before each wire-shaping step (refer to p. 58).

Create a ball end on one end of the wire. With roundnose pliers or your fingers, create a design that fits within the shape of the stone you are using (I formed a loose spiral) **[A]**. At some point in the design, the wire must meet itself (this point will be joined by solder). Estimate the length of wire you will need to reach around the stone, add any design elements, and cut the excess wire.

Place the wire shape on a tripod with mesh. Solder the first join using hard solder paste **[B]**. Quench in cool water.

With the excess wire you trimmed, make wire prongs to hold your stone. The shape and size of the stone will determine the number of prongs to use.

One method, shown below, is to make U shapes that will be long enough to reach

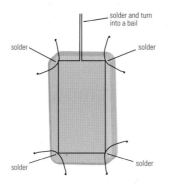

solder and turn into a bail

solder

solder

solder

solder

around the stone as prongs. Solder the base of each U to the center shape using medium paste solder **[C]**. (I used a soldering block for this step.) Quench and pickle.

The pendant pictured on p. 85 shows another variety of wire connection: I soldered two wires together and wrapped the ends around the stone to harness it.

When creating your harness for this project, you can build a bail into the wirework or you can shape and add a separate bail with solder.

This project polishes best in a rotary tumbler; if you polish by hand, you risk distorting the wires. Polish the harness (refer to The Basics: Polishing, p. 36).

Place the stone back into the wire harness and secure the stone with the tabs **[D]**. With chainnose pliers, tweak the wires as needed for a tight fit.

WIRE CONNECTIONS

SWEAT-SOLDERED SPIRALS

Pendulum earrings

These earrings look easy in theory, but making them match is a challenge. (You can always make a pendant instead.) Making anything in pairs will forever test your skills, especially when you have freehand shapes.

Create the cold project for more practice making spirals and learning how to duplicate shapes. In addition to these two skills, the hot project also will give you practice in recognizing how solder responds to heat and how it flows.

TOOLS & SUPPLIES
- flush wire cutters
- roundnose pliers
- chainnose pliers
- chasing hammer (optional)
- bench block (optional)
- pin vise or flex shaft
- 1mm drill bit (#56)

MATERIALS
- 24-gauge copper disks, 2 each 1" (25.5mm), .75" (19mm), .50" (13mm)
- 18-gauge sterling silver wire (or plated), 18" (45.7cm)
- pair of sterling silver earring wires

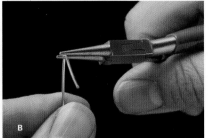

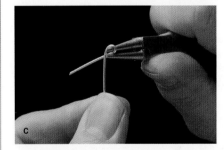

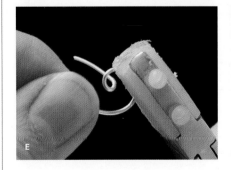

Cut two 3.5" (89mm), two 2" (51mm), and two 1.5" (38mm) pieces of 18-gauge wire. Using roundnose pliers, begin a spiral in one of the 3.5" wires, starting 1.25" (32mm) from one end **[A–C]**. Switch to chainnose pliers and grasp the short end of the wire. (You may also want to switch hands.)

With your other hand, gently turn the long end of the wire to make a spiral **[D]**. You may also opt to use nylon-jaw pliers **[E]**. After you have completed a couple of turns, use chainnose pliers to complete the turns. This will help create a tight spiral **[F]**. Using the largest disk as a gauge, tighten or loosen the spiral to make it fit within the disk. Repeat with the second wire.

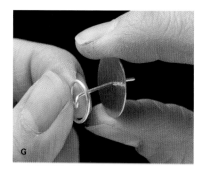

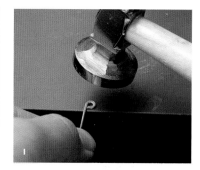

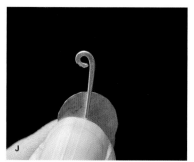

→ TIP To make your spirals look similar, keep track of where you start and make deliberate, repeated movements.

Continue making all of the spirals in the same way. It may help to mark the wires before spiraling: The 2" (51mm) spirals start 1.25" (32mm) from the end, and the 1.5" (38mm) spirals start 1" (25.5mm) from the end. Hammer the disks to add texture if desired.

Drill a hole in the center of all the disks using a pin vise or flex shaft.

Put the straight end of the largest spiral through the hole of the largest disk **[G]**. With chainnose pliers, make a sharp bend in the wire on the back of the disk **[H]**. For the largest disk, bend the wire

snug against the disk. For all subsequent disks, leave a little room for another wire to be attached.

At the end of the wire, create a simple loop with roundnose pliers. Hammer the loop flat on a bench block with a chasing hammer **[I, J]**. Repeat for all wire ends.

Interlock the wire loops to position the disks in descending size order **[K, L, M]**. Hammering the loops allows the pieces to lie flat.

Make a second earring. Attach the top wire of each earring to an earring wire.

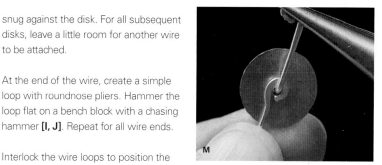

TOOLS & SUPPLIES
- wire cutters
- roundnose pliers
- chainnose pliers
- chasing hammer
- bench block
- 1.25mm hand punch
- soldering setup
- silver paste solder
- patina solution
- steel wool or polishing pad

MATERIALS
- 24-gauge copper or sterling silver disks, 2 each 1" (25.5mm), .75" (19mm), .5" (13mm)
- 18-gauge copper wire, 9" (22.9cm)
- 22-gauge copper wire, 7.5" (19.1cm)
- pair of earring wires

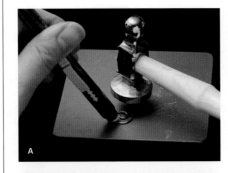

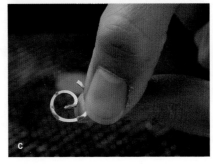

Cut two 2" (51mm), two 1.5" (38mm), and two 1" (25.5mm) pieces of 18-gauge wire. Make a spiral in each wire, using the first spiral of every pair as a pattern for the second. Hammer all the spirals flat with a chasing hammer on a bench block **[A]**. Flattening the spirals prepares them for soldering and creates a nice design **[B]**.

→ TIP Use the eraser end of a pencil to hold small pieces in place while hammering.

Pair the spirals with the appropriate-size disks. Place medium silver paste solder on the bottom of the spirals **[C]**. (If the solder shows a little under the copper spirals, the silver solder will blend in better to the silver base.) Solder the spiral to the disk **[D]**. Be sure to heat the disk well (not just the spiral) for a good attachment.

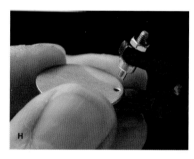

Cut two 1.5" (38mm), two 1.25", and two 1" pieces of 22-gauge copper wire. Hammer .25" (6.5mm) of one end of each wire flat to prepare for soldering **[E]**. Hammering the ends will help the wires lie flat and attach to the disks. Pairing the largest disk with the longest wire and so on, apply about 2mm of solder to the wire and solder to the back of each disk **[F, G]**.

Quench and pickle all of the pieces. Apply patina to all of the pieces. Polish with steel wool or a polishing pad. Pierce a hole at the bottom of the small and medium disks for the connection **[H]**. Make a plain loop on the end of each wire, connect the disks in descending size order, and then attach each earring unit to an earring wire.

REFERENCE CHARTS

Gauge conversion chart

AWG	inches	mm
6	0.162	4.11
7	0.1443	3.67
8	0.1285	3.26
9	0.1144	2.91
10	0.1019	2.59
11	0.0907	2.30
12	0.0808	2.05
14	0.0641	1.63
16	0.0508	1.29
18	0.0403	1.02
20	0.032	0.81
22	0.0254	0.65
24	0.0201	0.51
26	0.0159	0.40

Metal availability chart

Metal	Wire availability	Sheet availability	Mohs' scale for hardness
Sterling silver	X	X	3
Fine silver	X	X	2.5
Silver-filled	X	X	—
Nickel	X	X	4
Aluminum	X	X	2.75
Stainless steel	limited	limited	7+
Gold (karat)	X	X	3
Gold-filled	limited	very limited	—
Yellow brass	X	X	3
Red brass (bronze)	limited	limited	3
Copper	X	X	3

ACKNOWLEDGMENTS

Andy Gray – my dear husband, who still loves me despite my bad days. He finds the patience to continue to support all of my whims. I love you.

Zim Photography – my twin sister, who has put all of her passion for photography, skill, and knowledge into this project to create a beautiful body of work that we are both proud of.

Alex Ashley – my cheerleader. Thanks to Alex's enthusiasm and encouragement, I am where I am today in the teaching world. She was the first to believe in me.

Laura, Linda, Elliot, and "the boys" – my pit crew. They listen, they council, they make me laugh, and they do everything I just can't get to.

Jean Kanzinger – my personal portrait photographer. Not only did she make me look fantastic, she has been a terrific sounding board throughout this process.

Alison Pretious – our photo production assistant. She came all the way from England to help the process and was a tremendous asset, but more importantly, she mediated the twins' opinions.

Friends and students who have kept me level headed with my mission to explore jewelry and share my knowledge.

Main cover image and step-by-step photos by Zim Photography

FROM THE AUTHOR

Photo: Jean Kanzinger

My passion for designing jewelry began in the early '90s when I needed professional jewelry to look the part while working in management at Neiman Marcus, so I began making my own. Since then, my work in the jewelry industry has evolved from producing a line of jewelry that was featured in over 30 stores in the Midwest to operating retail bead supply stores to my current internet-based jewelry supply store, The Urban Beader.

Teaching people how to design and make jewelry was the next logical step as my store required more than just supplies. As customers became students, I found that I enjoyed teaching others how to make jewelry as much as I enjoyed creating it. Today I teach jewelry-making classes across the United States.

My sincere hope is that I will be able to share my knowledge with those seeking to learn more.

Continue your metalworking journey . . .

Helpful mini exercises for easy metal fabrication techniques serve as a springboard for 16 exciting projects that unite beads, gemstones, and metalwork in perfect harmony!

64407 • $21.95

Take the mystery out of soldering! Twelve finished projects with clear instructions make this the next-best thing to being in one of Joe's sold-out classes!

64063 • $21.95

Use metal shears and cold connections to cut metal from shaped templates and layer into delightful daffodils, orchids, roses, and more using easy-to-learn techniques.

64438 • $21.95

Ask for these books in your favorite bead or craft shop!

Or order at www.KalmbachStore.com or call 1-800-533-6644

Monday – Friday, 8:30 a.m. – 4:30 p.m. CST. Outside the United States and Canada call 262-796-8776, ext. 661.